CityCareerSeries.com

CityCareerSeries.com offers a multitude of high quality, concise and easy-to-understand tips, articles, videos and blogs:

- You will find information on boosting your employability, networking and the different types of firms and opportunities that you can apply for.
- The interactive (and syncable) calendar provides easy access to firm deadlines and links to application portals, whilst the firm profiles give you an insight into the range of City firms looking to hire graduates.
- You will find examples of application and interview questions that are typically encountered, complete with detailed suggestions of how to tackle them.
- Psychometric, situational judgement and e-tray tests are explained and techniques to help you approach them are suggested.
- Appropriate behaviour during internships is considered and hundreds of previous interns have offered an insight into their experiences whilst undertaking a variety of internships and placements at different City firms.
- Topical news stories are presented weekly, complete with explanations of why the stories may affect firms and their clients.
- Different industries have been analysed and the frameworks that can help you to conduct your own analysis of industries have been explained.
- An overview of the sources you should read to keep abreast of developments relevant to City firms and their clients has also been provided.

Social Media

 www.facebook.com/citycareerseries

 www.linkedin.com/company/city-career-series

 www.twitter.com/Career_Series

 City Career Series

Online Communities

Want to share tips and network with people at the same stage as you in the recruitment process?
Join one of our online communities!

- **Commercial Law Applicants**
  www.facebook.com/groups/commerciallawapplicants
- **Commercial Law Interns**
  www.facebook.com/groups/commerciallawinterns
- **Investment Banking & Finance Applicants**
  www.facebook.com/groups/investmentbankingandfinanceapplicants
- **Investment Banking & Finance Spring Interns**
  www.facebook.com/groups/investmentbankingandfinancespringinterns
- **Investment Banking & Finance Summer Interns**
  www.facebook.com/groups/investmentbankingandfinancesummerinterns
- **Operations, Risk & Compliance Applicants**
  www.facebook.com/groups/operationsriskandcomplianceapplicants
- **Technology Applicants**
  www.facebook.com/groups/technologyapplicants
- **Consultancy Applicants**
  www.facebook.com/groups/consultancyapplicants

Contents

Introduction

This handbook offers a range of hints and tips designed to help guide you through the recruitment process for a range of City careers. It includes an insight into the types of skills and strengths that firms will expect you to possess and advice on how you can try to accumulate experiences that facilitate your personal development. It guides you through application questions, CV structures, interview preparation and psychometric tests, right through to the importance of networking and how to approach internships. I have had the pleasure of delivering countless presentations over the past few years on the topics covered in this handbook alongside a wide variety of colleagues who have secured internships and jobs in a broad range of industries. I would like to thank all of them for their insights, which have contributed to my thinking and therefore to the content of this handbook.

There is no objectively *correct* way to approach applications, tests, interviews and internships. This handbook simply collates key pieces of advice that I would personally have found useful when first embarking upon my career pursuit and I recommend that you use it as a starting point from which you then engage in further research and preparation.

- I want to help you understand the ways in which you can boost your employability and make your answers stand out.

- I provide examples of the experiences, skills, strengths, capabilities and interests that many firms will expect candidates to have accumulated.

- I look at the types of questions firms can ask in order to ascertain the extent to which you have developed these competencies and strengths.

- I aim to help you really sell yourself by showing you how to draw out the key/valuable skills from the different experiences you have accumulated and show you how to back up the statements you make on application forms and during interviews with *evidence*.

However, you must remember that your experiences, competencies, application quality and interview technique are not the only elements firms consider. Top organisations expect strong academic performances at university, usually from the very beginning (especially Law firms), so make sure you study hard in your first year, even if it 'doesn't count' towards your degree classification. Moreover, not all firms approach recruitment identically. Some firms may reject an application if a single spelling mistake is found. Some may focus more on international experience or language abilities. Some may have higher thresholds for psychometric tests or expect higher university grades.

It is important that you never lie during interviews and that you are able to substantiate any statements you make. Recruiters are very skilled at noticing if you are trying to bluff your way through (you may be asked to provide a lot of detail when recounting experiences). Getting caught lying or overly-embellishing the truth reflects negatively upon your character and is likely to cause recruiters to question the other statements you have made. At the end of the day, they are looking to get to know *you*.

Note that this handbook started as a series of blog posts entitled 'Tip of the Week' on the City Career Series Facebook page. Keep checking the Facebook page and our website for updates to the information contained within this handbook, in addition to new articles.

A special thank you to Sarah Cockburn, without whose continuous support and advice this handbook may never have materialised. A huge thanks to the City Career Series team (Carly Schogger, Nowtash Alsafar and Chris Phillips) for their incredible hard work, creativity and enthusiasm. A massive thank you to Claire Leslie (Warwick Law School Careers Consultant) for her extensive edits and invaluable suggestions. Thanks also to Susan Vollmer for her fantastic work on the City Career Series videos and Anne Wilson for her advice relating to strengths-based questions. Thanks also to Christopher Stoakes for all his advice and support and for providing the inspiration for the City Career Series handbooks. Thanks to all those that have supported me throughout this project, in particular Danny Schogger, Poppy, Tomisin Mosuro, Alice Toop, Kai Majerus, Hugh Beale and the lawyers that I met whilst interning for all their lectures, inspiration, proof reading, comments and suggestions. Thanks to Sean McCaffrey and Philip Dekker for helping me find my way into commercial law and to Jasmine Schembri for involving me in the university society that inspired this handbook. Thank you to Vinay Mistry (vinay@vinaymistry.com) for designing citycareerseries.com and Chris Phillips (www.cphillipsdesign.uk) - who deserves a second mention - for his endless patience and fantastic graphic design work. Thanks to the members and the executive committee of Warwick Finance Societies for all the positive responses and useful feedback relating to earlier drafts of this handbook over the years.

Please note that the firms that have contributed to this handbook are only responsible for the information contained in their particular articles.

Where To Start?

If you are just starting out on your career path, the sheer number of industries, firms, divisions within firms and opportunities available to experience these firms can be quite overwhelming and confusing! You could start by trying to gain an insight into a range of careers and firms. Keep an open mind. Look at large firms, small firms, niche firms, corporations with in-house professional services teams and different industries. This will not only broaden your understanding of how the City works, but could also ensure that your future decisions are better informed. Remember, the City is not for everyone.

Note that opportunities offered by different organisations tend to target different student groups. Some opportunities are only available to those studying a particular degree and some are only open to students at a specific stage of their degree (or to graduates). In addition, some employers recruit on a rolling basis. This means that they assess candidates and make offers as and when they receive applications. Beware, as this leads to the real risk that spaces may fill up before the application deadline. Other recruiters read applications only once the deadline has passed, meaning it matters less when you submit your application. There is no point wasting time on an application only to discover that you are not eligible to apply or that all the places have been taken! Do your research before applying.

Opportunities: Year Of Study

- 1st years are generally offered brief insight opportunities at the organisation's offices (lasting from a few hours to 1 week). These typically involve little or no responsibility, but can (depending on the firm) lead to fast-track opportunities. At the very least they provide evidence of your research and commitment to the career and can therefore bolster your application for a full internship later on.

- Penultimate year students are typically offered longer internships (lasting 2 weeks – 10 weeks), which can involve real work, more responsibility and a range of assessments. For 2nd year students doing a 4 year degree, different firms take different approaches to what they are willing to offer. Check your eligibility for schemes very carefully.

- Some firms also offer internships to finalists and graduates, although other firms prefer finalists and graduates to apply directly for jobs.

- After graduation, some industries require candidates to continue with further study, either full-time for a limited period, or part-time whilst also working for the firm in order to prepare for additional examinations (for instance, accountants and actuaries).

Opportunities: Different Industries

Investment Banking

- Investment banks tend to offer Spring Weeks for 1st year students doing a 3-year degree and 2nd year students doing a 4-year degree. Spring Weeks typically include group exercises, a series of presentations and work shadowing opportunities, but will usually involve little or no responsibility. They can (depending on the firm) lead to fast-track opportunities.

- Full 10-12 week internships are then typically available for penultimate and final year students, although some internships on offer also cater to graduates. These internships typically involve candidates in real work (which can mean much longer working hours!) and candidates may also have to undertake a range of assessments throughout.

Commercial Law

- Commercial law firms tend to offer insight days for 1st year students, although a select few offer 2 day or week-long experiences. Some firms also offer open days for students at any stage in their education (including graduates). These opportunities may include work shadowing, group exercises and presentations from lawyers and graduate recruiters.

- Many firms then offer longer internships at Christmas, Easter and/or summer (timing can depend on whether you study Law and whether you are in your penultimate or final year of study). Candidates will usually sit in one or two departments during the internship and will have the opportunity to work with their supervisor and/or team on real work.

- If you receive a job offer, you will then have to complete the Legal Practice Course (LPC) followed by a period of "recognised professional training" (normally lasting for 2 years and referred to as a "training contract") before you become a qualified solicitor. Non-Law students will also have to complete the Graduate Diploma in Law (GDL) before embarking upon the LPC.

- Note that this may all change as early as the latter half of 2017 however. The Solicitors Regulation Authority (SRA) is currently consulting stakeholders on the possible introduction of a standardised "Solicitors Qualifying Examination" to replace the GDL and LPC.

Consultancy, Accountancy & Other Financial Services Firms

- Consultancy, accountancy and other financial services firms differ more in their approach. Some offer insight days/weeks catering for 1st years (for instance the PWC Talent Academy, the Accenture Boot Camp, the McKinsey Discover programme and the EY Leadership Academies). Longer internships are still generally reserved for students further along in their studies.

- As with commercial law and investment banking opportunities, shorter opportunities are likely to involve less responsibility (effectively giving *you* the opportunity to learn more about the firm and industry), whilst longer internships typically involve you in real work and give the firm the opportunity to assess *you* more carefully.

Other Opportunities

- You may also have access to informal insight opportunities offered by university societies. These tend to be less competitive and involve a less onerous application process, yet can still provide you with a valuable insight that can help to inform and shape your future career-decisions.

- Some firms also offer other opportunities that can help you to build a rapport with and gain a greater insight into those firms, in turn perhaps increasing your likelihood of securing internship/job interviews in the future. For instance, some firms recruit students who have just completed their first year to become campus ambassadors (a role for which you may get paid). Many firms are also anxious to increase their diversity, so if you are from an underrepresented socio-economic or ethnic background or are disabled, there may be special opportunities open to you.

- If you are at university, a great way to clarify which roles are open to you in light of your year and subject of study is to attend firm presentations or to visit your university career department. Alternatively, look at websites such as citycareerseries.com, thestudentlawyer.com, ratemyplacement.com, lawcareers.net and the websites of the firms to which you are considering applying.

We have supplemented the above section with a series of videos and articles outlining the opportunities available at commercial law firms, investment banks, consultancy firms and other professional services firms. The recruitment process for each type of firm is also covered. These videos and articles can be found at:

www.CityCareerSeries.com → Where To Start → Introduction to [relevant industry]

Boosting Your Employability

Firms want to recruit well-rounded individuals who have clearly developed relevant foundational skills. They will look at your participation in and experience of a range of activities across professional, academic and non-academic domains. If you only have academic experiences to demonstrate your competencies, this may not present you as a well-rounded individual and may suggest that you would not necessarily fit with the firm's culture or interact well with the firm's employees. Similarly, if you have only non-academic extracurricular experiences to draw from, a firm may doubt whether you have developed the ability to perform and interact with others within a professional setting.

I was rejected from my very first interview (years ago!) as the interviewer felt that I had not accumulated a broad enough range of experiences. This was because I had provided only non-academic examples to evidence my skill development during a competency interview.

Try to accumulate a range of experiences and positions of responsibility and get involved in university societies and university (or local) clubs and initiatives. You'll probably have a great time doing so anyway! Ask yourself, is your university in any way *different* because you have been there? Have *your* contributions enhanced the experience(s) of other students?

We have supplemented this section with a series of videos and articles relating to boosting your employability. These can be found at:

www.CityCareerSeries.com → Where To Start? → Boosting Your Employability

Work Experience

If you have undertaken work experience, regardless of whether it is paid or unpaid, as an intern in a professional services firm or as an office assistant or shop assistant, this will boost your employability. You will be able to demonstrate that you have a strong work ethic, you are able to commit to an organisation and that you have accumulated some experience interacting with clients, working in a team with colleagues, adhering to deadlines and balancing multiple responsibilities.

Have you worked in the family business? Have you worked in customer services, perhaps as a checkout assistant or a bartender? Have you already visited firms in the industry to which you are applying (even if only for a few hours or for an informal office visit)? I listed working in a small office, working in the music industry, completing a paper round and working at Waitrose (pushing trolleys) as examples of my previous work experience (alongside more relevant industry experience, such as firm office visits). Many firms liked these examples as they felt that this demonstrated that I had a strong work ethic and that my decision to embark upon a highly pressurised career was better informed as a result of the comparison that such work experiences provided.

Try to gain an insight into a range of different careers. This should broaden your understanding of how the City works, whilst also ensuring your personal decisions and career choices are better informed. Keep an open mind as you may well have preconceptions about various industries that are not necessarily reflective of the reality of working within them.

For instance, I have many friends who started out thinking they wanted to work in one industry only to decide (having gained experience in a variety of different organisations) that they in fact wanted to work in quite another. Others have decided that they would be happier working for small, niche, or regional firms instead of large City firms, or for a department within a corporation.

Making The Most Of Holidays

If you have not secured an internship, or have an internship that takes up only a proportion of your summer, start thinking about how best to use any free time you may have. Many firms in interviews will ask how you have spent your 3 – 4 month break and 'watching TV' is never a great answer! Use this time to do something interesting – something that sets you apart from other candidates – as this in turn will provide firms with an insight into your character. Are you the kind of person who uses your initiative and drive to actively pursue your passions and interests? Are you committed to personal development? Do you have a desire to experience different cultures?

You could directly ask firms in the industry you are aiming to work in for work experience. Cold calling and emailing *can* work, although it is best to start by utilising any contacts you may have. Family, friends and friends of family may be able to help out, as may university staff. Universities may even offer grants to assist their students, for instance social mobility schemes for certain student demographics or bursaries for high performing students. Do not be afraid to ask!

There are formal internships and programmes that also look great on your CV and can be a lot of fun. Google the Study India and Study China programmes. Consider working at a summer camp (through agencies such as Camp America). There are also a broad range of volunteering and charity initiatives, both domestically and abroad, that could provide unique and interesting experiences, whilst also enhancing your employability.

If instead of formal or informal work placements you decided to spend your summer travelling, this can also provide a fantastic topic of conversation in interviews and again presents you as a motivated individual with an interest in experiencing different cultures. It is important to remember that once you embark upon your career, you will no longer have the opportunity to travel for extended periods of time.

Travelling can help you to develop a wide range of skills, most notably your confidence, ability to adapt to different cultures, your interpersonal skills, and your ability to organise and manage time effectively (especially if you are travelling around a continent with questionable transport links!). Travelling also shows that you are willing to place yourself outside of your comfort zone. However, supplement travel with other activities and work experience in order to present yourself as a well-rounded individual.

Alternatively, you could take a summer job or start a project (for instance, found a small business or do something creative). This can reflect positively on your personal motivation, work ethic and interests. City Career Series began as an extracurricular project whilst I was at university.

Academic & Commercial Activities

Consider joining and actively participating in academic societies. Your university may well have a Commercial Law, Finance, Debating or Business society you could join, or, of course, your degree subject society. If your membership leads to you attending particularly interesting presentations or participating in skill-enhancing interactive case studies, then you could use these experiences as examples to demonstrate to firms that you put your free time to good use.

Participation in the likes of Young Enterprise, Duke of Edinburgh, Model United Nations or interactive business challenges/case studies could also reflect well on your character, so perhaps sign up for initiatives such as these if you have not yet already accumulated similar experiences. Particular modules or group work exercises that you have undertaken whilst studying can also provide interesting talking points during interviews and deliver an insight into how you have developed your knowledge and capabilities.

In order to demonstrate my academic extracurricular activities I listed my membership of various commercial societies and my involvement in the Study India and Study China programmes. I also talked about my engagement in team-based business modules at university and participation in firm business challenges on campus.

Positions Of Responsibility

Firms need to know that their employees can effectively take on responsibility and subsequently manage their time effectively to ensure tasks are completed to the standard required and within the deadlines set. Undertaking positions of responsibility at university whilst maintaining a strong academic performance is a fantastic way to demonstrate that you can do this.

Try to join the executive committee of the university societies and clubs in which you are most interested. It does not matter whether it is the Finance Society, Music Theatre Society, Ice Hockey Club or a charitable society. It doesn't matter whether you are a 1st year representative, President, Club Captain or Head of Marketing. The premise is the same: these experiences give you scope to prove to firms that you have the ability to handle responsibility and to demonstrate what you are capable of achieving if given the chance.

Find out when elections are taking place, as these are usually open to anyone wishing to apply. Getting to know the current executive committee and members of a society and demonstrating your interest in getting involved (by attending events, offering to help and asking the current executive committee about their particular roles) could help to give you a better chance of getting elected or appointed.

If at school you were selected as a Prefect, Ambassador or Head Boy/Girl or you were elected/appointed onto some sort of student liaison or event committee, these count as positions of responsibility. If you have ever taught or mentored (be it Maths, Music, English or Dance) this can similarly evidence how you have developed certain skills.

The same applies if you are/were a firm's campus ambassador (and it is perfectly fine to state this on applications to rival firms; if anything, it validates you as a worthy candidate as you passed the recruitment process implemented by another firm). I listed: drum kit teacher, founder of a (casual) 5-a-side football team, my role as campus ambassador for a City firm and my role as President of the Commercial Law Society (and later, Warwick Finance Societies) among my positions of responsibility.

These are just a few examples. All of your experiences may be relevant and go to show that you are the sort of person who gets involved. With a little creativity and open-mindedness, you can draw a surprising number of skills out of each experience. For instance, I was once asked to demonstrate a time during which I had demonstrated commercial awareness. You could approach such a question simply by giving an example of how your experiences provided an insight into the fundamental business processes that help to create value, for example: customer service, branding, marketing, pricing products, effective management, efficient operations etc. You do not need to have been the CEO to make such observations!

Other Extracurricular Activities

It is easy to get involved in non-academic extracurricular activities, at least on a casual basis and at a non-competitive level. You can be a complete beginner. For instance, I was never good enough to get into the official university football team, but this did not stop me setting up a 5-a-side football team.

Try to demonstrate that you have a range of interests and the motivation and initiative to pursue them. Are you willing to remove yourself from your comfort zone and try something new?

Dancing / Acting

- Do you like to perform on stage or on film? Have you taken part in university theatre productions or dance competitions? This could demonstrate that you have developed the confidence, presentation skills and team working abilities required to succeed in a client-led industry.

Sport

- Do you play for the university netball team? Do you play in (or manage) a casual 5-a-side team? Do you enjoy horse riding? Have you run a marathon or climbed a mountain? Do you enjoy diving, skiing or playing table tennis? Have you pursued these interests through joining a club?

- Attending regular training sessions or regularly involving yourself in a particular sport could demonstrate your ability to commit, your determination, your ability to motivate yourself and others and your time management abilities. If you have done something particularly interesting and unique, mention it! I mentioned that I had gone cage diving with great white sharks, which again provided an interesting talking point during interviews.

Music / Art

- Do you play an instrument? Do you play in a rock band or the university big band? Do you like to sing at open "mic" nights? Do you paint, make videos or engage in graphic design? If so, this could demonstrate that you have the creativity sought after by top City firms (which are regularly required by clients to provide innovative solutions to unique problems). If you are doing these activities with others, this could also enable you to demonstrate teamwork.

Volunteering / Charity

- Have you raised money for charity, helped at an orphanage, been involved in school or university charitable initiatives or volunteered at music festivals? This could demonstrate your desire to work for a firm that offers volunteering opportunities (for instance, pro bono legal work), whilst also showing that you are an ethical person. It can also provide interesting anecdotes for interviews.

- For instance, I volunteered for the Glastonbury Festival 'Recycling Crew' for many years, which effectively involved taking a position as an unpaid bin man. However, it was great fun, I met a broad range of people and I accumulated some great experiences to draw from when answering application and interview questions.

- If you talk a lot about volunteering in your application/interview, demonstrate that your statements are genuine by getting involved if given the chance during an internship. I got involved in various charitable initiatives during internships and this helped to substantiate the statements that I had previously made.

- A note of caution: avoid suggesting that your decision to apply to a particular City organisation was based primarily upon the volunteering opportunities on offer to its employees. Volunteering opportunities are nice "add-ons" that can help to enhance your working experience and do not provide part of the core business of City professional services firms. City employers want to know that you are keen to help them make money and/or improve performance. After all, these firms are businesses, not charities (no matter how much they may focus on their altruistic side during presentations).

Travel

- Have you studied abroad or travelled to interesting places? Have you completed a ski season or been on a university trip abroad? Have you participated in "Jailbreak" (this is a charity initiative run by societies at many universities which involves attempting to get as far away from your university campus in 36 hours without spending any money)?

- If so, remember to explain *why/how* this has made you more suitable for the role. Such experiences could evidence: your ability to adapt to different cultures, organise yourself effectively and remain positive whilst under pressure; your desire to work in an international setting; and that you are an interesting, open-minded individual.

Reading, Research & Preparation

Preparation is key. Completing strong applications can take a great deal of time, as can preparing sufficiently for interviews and internships. I have heard many examples of people being offered interviews with only a couple of days' notice, so start preparing as early as possible. There are many useful sources you can read well in advance of making applications, attending interviews or undertaking internships in order to boost your commercial awareness and ensure you acquire the knowledge required to succeed. Many candidates ask how many applications they should send out, but there is no definitive answer. The number should depend on:

1. How much time you are willing to put in

Sending out 3 or 4 thoroughly researched and well written applications is more likely to result in you being offered interviews than if you send out 100 poorly researched, badly written applications.

2. How competitive it is to get the job for which you are applying

If 1 in 20 applicants get a place, you should consider hedging your bets and sending out a number of applications (perhaps 5-10 of *high quality*). Even if you believe you tick all the boxes, applying to only one firm is a risky strategy, as that firm may have particular requirements that you do not meet. Be realistic. If firms state they only accept applications from candidates with top grades or extensive experience, consider whether you meet these criteria and if not, focus your efforts elsewhere.

We have supplemented this section with a series of videos and articles relating to application and interview preparation. These can be found at:

www.CityCareerSeries.com → Applications & Interviews → Preparation

Writing Applications

If you have not yet made applications, perhaps visit your university's career department and/or meet with friends and family members if they have experience applying to or working in similar firms. They may be able to provide an insight into what firms are expecting from your application answers (although bear in mind that their insights may be distinctly less helpful if they work in completely different industries).

It can be really beneficial to have your applications checked by multiple sources over an extended period (whilst making improvements along the way). You are probably more likely to miss mistakes or structural issues than a person taking a fresh look at your application. After proof reading their own work multiple times, people tend to read what they *think* they wrote as opposed to what they *actually* wrote.

This is something that happened to me over and over again whilst writing this handbook. I learnt to accept any help I was offered from people willing to proof read sections. Career departments tend to offer application checks as one of their services. Use them!

In addition, look out for firm presentations on campus that relate to the application process. Who better to secure advice from than the firm to which you are applying? You may have to sign up for these presentations in advance, so check whether this is the case. Some firms make a note of who attends, so if you plan on claiming in an interview that you were at a particular presentation, make sure you actually go!

Interview Preparation

Consider your skills, abilities, strengths and weaknesses well in advance of applications and interviews. An excellent way to prepare is to list out all the experiences you have accumulated and really consider all the possible skills that you could draw out from them. Questions can be quite specific at times, for instance I was asked to detail a time when I had worked in a team and had to deal with a colleague that was not pulling their weight.

Listing out your experiences and skills in advance will ensure that you are less likely to forget about experiences that are worth discussing at a later stage, which can be especially useful if you are asked questions that catch you off guard. It also enhances the likelihood of you being able to draw from a wide range of experiences whilst under pressure to answer a lot of questions in a short space of time. In addition, try to meet with people who have already been through the interview process at the firms you are applying to. They may be able to provide an insight into the types of questions that the firms may ask. You can also attempt to research the types of question that firms have previously asked candidates online.

Commercial Knowledge & Current Affairs

As part of your assessment, you may have to complete case studies or interviews involving topics such as: business performance, financing deals, mergers & acquisitions, investment options and the role of the firm/different departments. The other City Career Series handbooks can provide you with a solid grounding in the technical concepts you may be required to apply when tackling interview case studies and work set during internships. There are editions available that focus on commercial law, investment banking and consultancy. Christopher Stoakes has also written a number of highly recommended books on commercial awareness. See the *Further Reading* section for more detail.

In addition, get into the habit of reading the news daily, if only for a few minutes. You will soon build a comprehensive knowledge and understanding of what is going on in the business areas relevant to the organisations to which you are applying.

We have produced a series of articles explaining and analysing topical current affairs. Read these at:

www.CityCareerSeries.com → Commercial Awareness → Topical Current Affairs

We produce weekly topical news summaries, which can be viewed at:

www.CityCareerSeries.com → Commercial Awareness → Headlines

Subscribe to our mailing list to receive these news summaries by email. You can do this at:

www.CityCareerSeries.com → Connect → Sign Up

Firm News

Even if you are not applying to or interviewing at a particular firm for a while, researching the firm in advance and keeping up to date with its deals and announcements could hold you in good stead if you are later required to discuss your motivation for wanting to work at the firm in depth.

Read the firm's annual review, news stories on its website and general news articles that mention the firm (Google can be a good place to start). Perhaps subscribe to firm newsletters. Read The Lawyer, the Financial Times, the Economist or one of the many other sources that report on deals and general firm news. Some of these sources let you subscribe to free email digests that can help to keep you abreast of firm, industry and topical news. You might also want to follow organisations on Twitter and Facebook, as employers have been known to check to see if you have followed or liked them!

Networking

The City is a small place and networking is a useful and important skill to develop if you are planning to embark upon a City career. Your network should not only be comprised of people working in the same office as you. Consider the fact that some of your friends, school and university colleagues, family members and friends of family members will work at different firms and in other industries that are still very relevant to your chosen firm/career. For instance, bankers, lawyers, accountants, consultants, corporations and government officials regularly work together on deals, as do those working in your firm's international offices.

We have supplemented this section with a series of videos and articles relating to networking. These can be found at: **www.CityCareerSeries.com → Where To Start? → Networking**

How Can Networking Benefit You?

People within your network (or people you meet through networking) may be able to provide advice about a range of different careers based on their own experiences. They may help you to secure work experience or assist you with writing applications and preparing for interviews. They can help you to make informed decisions (for instance when deciding which firm to choose if you are lucky enough to receive multiple offers) and provide general advice relating to your training and the work that you will be set once you start.

More importantly, it is likely that you will end up working with or for people within your network throughout your career and networking from an early stage can help to ensure that you have the best possible working relationships with future colleagues. Working with or for someone with whom you have already built a relationship may be more enjoyable and effective than working with someone with whom you have not yet had the opportunity to build a rapport. Accumulating a large network of contacts is likely to be very beneficial. People within your network are arguably more likely to make reasonable concessions (e.g. if they are working on the opposite side of a deal) and work with you efficiently to get the job done. Moreover, as you progress into more senior positions, you will rely on your network to attract new work and clients to the firm. If you have proven yourself to people and built up solid relationships, these people are in turn more likely to want to work with you in the future (rather than people they do not know from other firms).

If you decide to pursue a career change – either to join a different office within your firm's global network of offices, a different firm within the same industry, or a different type of firm altogether – your networks may be essential in helping you to discover the opportunities available and to get a foot in the door. Doing a good job for and keeping in touch with clients and colleagues you have worked with can help you to do this. The longer your history with these people stretches back, the more likely it is that they will be willing to help you out (assuming you have consistently left a strong impression). Accordingly, try to network from the earliest possible stage.

How Can You Network?

Social Media

LinkedIn (and social media in general) provides a good starting point. Look to see whether friends, family members, teachers/lecturers, or university alumni have industry experience or career-interests relating to yours. If they do, there is no harm in connecting with them. However, ensure you write a personalised message when you request to connect with them, explaining your reasons for doing so and how you know (of) them. More senior professionals may well receive hundreds of connection requests per month. Failing to personalise a request can make you appear lazy and unprofessional (or even rude) and may result in your request being ignored.

Make sure that your LinkedIn is business-like, up-to-date, well presented and free from spelling and grammatical errors and that your photograph is recent and professional. For people you have never met before, your profile will provide their first impression of you.

University

You could try to contact people at your university who have secured internships or jobs and ask whether they would be willing to meet over coffee and provide guidance. University societies may well provide such opportunities for you. Join relevant societies and get involved! Work on building relationships with those you meet. If a contact helps you and you secure a job, message them to thank them and keep them informed. Similarly if you find out someone at your school or university has secured a job at the same firm as you, get in touch *before* you start work in order to start building that relationship.

If you have successfully secured a job, be open to helping out other students with their career pursuits. You may well end up working with them in the future. They are unlikely to forget the guidance they have received, which may in turn help to ensure a positive working relationship exists in the future (even if you are on opposite sides of a transaction).

Joining commercially-oriented university societies may also provide ample opportunities to meet firms that sponsor those societies. You could offer to help societies to arrange or promote firm events, which in turn will afford you the opportunity to demonstrate to these firms (and to the society's executive committee) that you are a professional, reliable and well-organised individual. This could also provide you with opportunities to gain an insight into firms and might help you further down the line if you stand for election into the society's executive committee. This could in turn enable you to set yourself apart from other candidates when answering interview and application questions.

Firm events

Attend careers fairs and campus presentations at your university in addition to firm office visits where possible. This will provide you with opportunities to gain an insight into a variety of different firms and interact with their employees. Such events could provide you with unique and essential information and anecdotes that can in turn help you to explain your motivation for applying to the firm(s) in your applications and during interviews. However, research the firms beforehand and formulate strong questions that will help you to gain a better insight into elements such as the firm's culture, its challenges and its approach to training. Demonstrating such research may well impress the people with whom you interact, allowing you to evidence that you have a strong interest in the firm.

Why not request the email addresses of the people you talk to? Message them after the event to thank them for their time, thereby reminding them of your name. If you have created a strong first impression, this may well help you progress through to the interview stage as some firms tend to flag impressive candidates on their system after meeting them in person. I benefitted enormously from meeting a variety of firms (and their employees) at countless campus presentations, career fairs and office visits. Some employees may even be willing to provide further advice after the event (although do not be too pushy, these people are generally very busy).

CVs & Cover Letters

There is no objectively 'correct' way in which to structure CVs and cover letters. Different firms in different industries will have different preferences. It is worth undertaking additional research in order to ascertain exactly what the firms you are applying to expect. This section simply provides some basic pointers that you may want to consider. Avoid lying or overly embellishing the truth. You risk getting caught out, which in turn will reflect negatively upon your character and may cause the firm to question all the other statements you have made. Avoid being too generic and tailor your application to the particular role/firm in question.

CVs

Bear in mind that whilst a majority of financial services firms tend to expect one page CVs, some (especially law firms) prefer two page CVs. Some firms do not request CVs at all. Before starting to draft your CV, check what the firm to which you are applying expects and perhaps utilise your network to source examples of CVs that have helped applicants in the past to secure interviews. CVs provide an insight into your past experiences and achievements and evidence your writing style, your ability to distil information into short, concise sentences, your skill at structuring documents and your attention to detail. Do not be afraid to include more interesting or unique interests and experiences if you have space, as this can help you to stand out.

Avoid spelling and grammatical mistakes (and ask people to proof read your CV for you). Make sure your headings, dates, bullet points and font are in a consistent format and properly aligned. Your layout should look professional: avoid the use of flowery borders, bright colours and cartoon images (it happens!). Make sure the structure is clear and really outlines your experiences and achievements, even on a quick skim. Recruiters are unlikely to pour over your CV for long (evidence suggests that on the first look through a CV, employers give it attention for no more than 30 seconds). You could split your CV into sections, including for instance:

Personal Details
Name, address, phone number, email address, LinkedIn

Education
Include your secondary school and university

Relevant Work Experience
Finance, legal, accountancy, consultancy (etc.) work experience

Other Work Experience
Other paid work and internship-style experience

Positions Of Responsibility
e.g. Head Boy/Girl, university society executive committee etc.

Extracurricular Activities
Sport, music, art, drama, charity work, debating, dance, MUN

Additional Skills, Interests & Awards
Scholarships, prizes, certifications, music grades etc.

Use space wisely, especially if your CV is only one page long. Filling the page with large headings and including bullet points that contain only a couple of words could suggest you have little to say about yourself. Conversely, keep your sentences concise and to the point and avoid repetition.

Cover Letters

As with CVs, there is no objectively correct way in which to structure cover letters. Some firms may set word or character limits. Others may simply ask you to attach a separate document. Cover letters for established graduate schemes at large City firms should probably include an overview of your reasons for making the application and an insight into why you believe you are a suitable candidate. Cover letters for other types of roles may require greater emphasis on your competencies. Research into what is expected for the particular role for which you are applying.

Bear in mind that making speculative applications for casual work experience can call for a very different technique than that required when making full-time job applications. For example, if you are applying for experience at a small high street firm, you will not necessarily need to spend ages distinguishing it from similar employers in the same street. Approach your application from the basis of 'what I can do for you' rather than 'what you can do for me'.

Cover letters should be fairly concise (usually one page) and should be well written (accurate spelling and grammar) with a strong structure. After all, this may well provide the firm with its first impression of the standard of work that you are able to deliver. Whilst drafting your cover letter, using temporary headings can help to ensure you maintain a clear structure. Below is a structure favoured by some (including me) for cover letters for established graduate schemes at large City firms.

Mr/Mrs Your Name
Your Address
Your Phone Number
Your Email Address

Mr/Mrs Name Of Recruiter
Firm's Name
Firm's Address

Date

1. **Salutation (Dear…)**
   - Try to find the name of the specific person that will be receiving your application. This shows good research and professionalism. Otherwise, use 'Dear Sir/Madam'.

2. **Heading**
   - Summarise to purpose of the letter using a bold heading between the salutation and the introduction, e.g. '**Summer Internship Application**'.

3. **Introduction**
   - State the role/opportunity for which you are applying.

4. **State your reasons for applying for the job**
   - Tell the story of how your interest in your chosen career has developed.
   - See the 'Career Motivation' section of this handbook for help with this step.

5. **State your reasons for applying to the particular firm**
   - Do not give generic reasons for applying to that firm that merely reflect a quick skim of the firm's marketing materials. Think of legitimate ways to differentiate the firm and more importantly, relate these elements back to you in order to convince recruiters that these factors genuinely appeal.
   - See the 'Firm Motivation' section of this handbook for help with this step.

6. **Explain why you believe that you are a suitable candidate**
   - Relate your skills to the competencies required for the role in question and briefly explain how your strengths and experiences will add value/be advantageous to the organisation.
   - See the 'Competencies & Strengths' section of this handbook for help with this step.

7. **Conclusion**
   - You could thank the reader for considering your application before signing off. Sign off with "Yours sincerely" if you know the name of the reader, or 'Yours faithfully' if you do not.

Application & Interview Questions

The recruitment process for City careers can involve an application stage, psychometric testing, a phone or Skype/video interview and an assessment centre at the firm's offices. These stages are designed to test your strengths, capabilities and suitability to the role for which you are applying. There are five key elements that firms tend to focus on when setting application questions and interviewing candidates. These include:

Competencies, Strengths & Experience

- Firms will want to gain an insight into the skills and capabilities you have developed through your studies and extracurricular activities.

- Remind yourself of your personal experiences, positions of responsibility and extracurricular involvement. Focus on the skills and abilities you have developed.

Career Motivation

- Firms will want to understand your motivation for pursuing your career of choice.

- Consider how your experiences have influenced your decision to pursue your desired career.

Firm Motivation & Research

- Firms will want to know your reasons for wanting to work for them.

- Research the firm at which you are interviewing in depth so that you are able to differentiate it from its competitors and explain why these differentiating factors particularly appeal to you.

Current Affairs & The Professional Services Industry

- Firms may want to see evidence of your interest in and understanding of current affairs and the industry you are looking to work in.

- Build up your knowledge and understanding of current affairs to evidence your interest in the wider economy. Relate your knowledge to your prospective employer, its clients and the markets in which they operate. You should also research the challenges the industry is facing and assess proposed solutions.

Commercial Knowledge

- Firms may test your commercial knowledge (firm expectations will of course vary depending on the job you are applying for). As part of your assessment, you may have to complete case studies, give presentations and/or answer questions that typically focus on business issues and how a firm can assist its clients. This may involve consideration of: a business' performance, financing, mergers & acquisitions, investment options and the role of firms/different departments.

- For instance, if a client is considering purchasing another firm, what are the different financing options and the corresponding advantages and disadvantages of each? How can such a transaction be structured? What are the primary risks and how can they be mitigated? How can the firm help? These types of questions are covered in the City Career Series Commercial Law, Investment Banking and Consultancy Handbooks.

- Develop your business, finance and (where relevant) legal knowledge so that you can demonstrate and apply strong commercial logic during case studies and commercial awareness interviews. Do not just regurgitate definitions. Demonstrate an ability to flexibly apply the concepts to the facts of the case study provided and assess in that particular case which concepts are likely to be the most relevant and effective.

When preparing for interviews, I created separate documents for each of these elements (competencies, strengths & experience; firm motivation; career motivation; current affairs; and commercial knowledge) and highlighted the documents on the morning of each interview, much like revising for an exam. All the elements tend to be relevant (at least to some extent) to most City interviews. Once you have covered these elements in detail, it should therefore take less time to prepare for subsequent interviews. However, ensure you tailor your preparation depending on the firm you are interviewing at (and the role you are applying for).

Throughout interviews, firms will in addition look for composure, confidence, clear articulation, strong interpersonal skills and enthusiasm. Try to keep calm and do not be afraid to disagree with interviewers, so long as you can justify your comments and are sure you are not objectively wrong! Below is a brief summary of how you should look to prepare for each interview element.

Structuring Application & Interview Answers

Your application and interview answers will of course vary depending on the particular question. However, regardless of the question, your structure should be clear. It is advisable to draft application answers with temporary headings in place to ensure your answers remain logical and coherent. If you are discussing your motivation for wanting to work at the firm, do not mention training at the start, in the middle *and* at the end of your answer. Perhaps have a section dedicated to the development of employees, thus avoiding the risk of repeating yourself and coming across as unable to write concisely and coherently.

For scenario-based questions, for instance 'what is the biggest challenge you have faced?', 'detail a time when you have worked successfully in a team?' or 'detail a time when you have successfully undertaken a leadership role', the STAR (situation – task – action – result) approach to answering questions could be worth bearing in mind.

Situation

- Start by setting the scene, for instance: 'whilst running the university Finance Society…'. If you are discussing your biggest challenge, explain *why* the circumstances posed a challenge. If you are answering a question on teamwork, explain what led to you joining the team. For a question on leadership, explain how you ended up in a leadership position.

Task

- Follow by detailing your (or your team's) designated task and/or role, for instance: 'my team was tasked with arranging a ball for 400 people…'.

Action

- This is the most substantial part of the answer and requires you to explain what *you* actually did to complete the task, how you went about doing it, why you did it/why it was a challenge (etc.) and the skills you used/developed whilst taking such action. Remember that the employer has little interest in what others did and accordingly, when you are dealing with a teamwork question, try to avoid repeatedly using 'we'.

Result

- Conclude by explaining the impact your actions had and what you actually managed to achieve. Be prepared to discuss what you learned and could have done differently/improved upon.

When writing applications, draft your answers in a separate Microsoft Word Document. If the employer's website crashes (and they do), you will thus not lose your answers. It also makes it easier for you to use elements of your answers for other applications. Microsoft Word has a spelling and grammar check too, which the application form may not. Do no fully rely on this however as sometimes autocorrect may change a word or phrase in a manner than you had not wanted it to.

Competencies & Strengths

Firms generally emphasise the skills that they most value during campus presentations and office visits and on their websites. Although many firms stress similar skills, some firms may place greater emphasis on one or two particular skills or values. Different firms (and even different interviewers within the same firm) take very different approaches to competency interviews.

Some may ask ethical questions (e.g. 'would you ever pay a ransom?' or 'have you ever done anything ethically questionable?'). Others may focus more on strengths-based questions (e.g. 'what motivates you?' or 'what are your weaknesses?'). Organisations may alternatively assess your skill development through evaluating your contribution/reaction in different scenarios (e.g. 'when have you successfully led a team through a difficult situation?').

Make sure you do your research beforehand to deduce which skills and strengths you are likely to be required to address during your interviews and think about which of your experiences would be best to draw upon as examples. As part of your interview preparation, ensure that you know exactly what you wrote in your application and be prepared to talk at length about any of the experiences to which you have referred. If you have stated that you are proficient in a different language, make sure you remember how to speak it! I have heard stories of interviewers suddenly switching to a different language mid-interview to check whether the candidate really could speak the language(s) they claimed to know. If you have studied abroad, make sure you remember which modules you took. If you are an international student, be prepared to explain why you decided to study abroad and the research you undertook to inform that decision.

It is good to use a range of different examples in your applications and interviews, both academic and non-academic. This can help to demonstrate that you are a well-rounded individual. Try to demonstrate how your interests, experiences, competencies and strengths are relevant to the role for which you are applying and why they make you an ideal candidate. For instance, if you have worked in a supermarket, this could demonstrate work ethic, commitment and experience dealing with clients (clients are essentially customers), whilst evidencing that you have developed soft skills such as problem solving (if things have gone wrong) and negotiating.

Helpful preparation can include listing out all the interesting and/or relevant experiences that you have accumulated. Include positions of responsibility you have held, societies and sports teams you have been involved with, interesting group projects you have undertaken at university, part-time jobs and work experience in industries relevant to the organisation to which you are applying. Consider the particular skills and strengths that could be drawn out of each. You should then be ready for competency-based questions.

Why Key Competencies Are Relevant

Below is a guide to the key competencies and strengths firms tend to expect from candidates and why these competencies are required. Use these as a starting point and consider how your own experiences have helped you to develop them. You could reference some of these skills and capabilities when answering application questions.

Teamwork

- City employees regularly work in teams with internal colleagues and with clients and other firms. Organisations will therefore expect you to demonstrate that you are a strong team player, eager to contribute and able to listen to and encourage others.

Leadership ability

- As you progress through your career, you are likely to move into a more managerial role involving, for instance, responsibility for training junior employees. Firms therefore tend to value leadership experience.

Analytical ability

- City transactions regularly require the analysis of copious amounts of complicated data. Such analysis can facilitate financial planning and/or help City workers to formulate advice for clients.

Attention to detail

- Strong attention to detail is of vital importance, whether you are drafting contracts, inputting figures into financial models, drafting emails to clients or proof reading documents for supervisors. Small mistakes could lead clients (or supervisors) to perceive the firm (and/or you) as unprofessional, whilst larger mistakes could potentially give rise to a whole host of legal and financial issues for clients.

Organisation and time-management skills

- City workers are typically expected to juggle multiple projects for a number of clients at the same time. It is essential that they remain aware of all relevant deadlines (which can change at a moments notice) and keep up to date with any changes in those deadlines. Organisation and time-management skills are absolutely essential. Start by arriving on time for an interview!

Interpersonal skills

- City work typically involves ample contact with other professionals. Firms will want to know that you will interact positively with colleagues and contribute positively to the firm's culture. It is also essential that you will be able to be professional and effective when representing the firm to clients and in your dealings with other organisations with which the firm cooperates.

Ability to think laterally and innovatively

- Top City firms charge substantial amounts for their services. Increasingly, clients are instructing them only when they have particularly challenging and unique issues to resolve or strategies to execute. Firms want candidates that are able to think creatively and laterally to ensure client problems are tackled effectively.

Adaptability and flexibility

- City workers may be expected to work for and interact with a broad range of people who approach work in very different ways. Cultural awareness, including an ability to adapt your working style and the way you present yourself when necessary, can be essential. In addition, working hours and deadlines can be unpredictable. Candidates may have to demonstrate that they are willing to remain flexible with their time and travel.

Networking

- As you become more senior, you may be expected to bring work into the firm and this is often facilitated through networking. An ability to make connections and build relationships is therefore essential.

Communication skills, presentation skills and confidence

- Many City careers involve presenting to and regularly liaising with clients, other firms and employees within your firm. Confidence and communication skills are essential, as is an ability to deliver engaging, professional and concise presentations.

Motivation & ambition

- City work can be very demanding. Firms look for candidates able to rise to the challenge and excel. Demonstrating a commitment to personal development may help to show that you are such a candidate.

Commitment

- Firms want to know that you will stick around even when long hours and less interesting tasks arise. Demonstrating that you have been able to commit to tasks in the past can help you to prove that you are a worthy candidate.

Negotiation

- An ability to negotiate can be an essential skill. It is important if you are a lawyer negotiating contractual clauses, a consultant negotiating deadlines or a director in an investment bank negotiating fees.

Ability to work under pressure

- Where deadlines are impending and things go wrong, City careers can involve working under a lot of pressure in order to meet client expectations. Think about times when you have excelled under pressure in the past.

Common Competency Questions

Competency questions tend to focus upon your ability to showcase the skills that are necessary to succeed in your chosen career. These are usually assessed through asking that you talk about past situations in which you have developed or demonstrated the relevant skills.

Typical questions you may be asked:

1. **Technical skills:** when have you had to pay close attention to detail? Discuss a time when you have had to negotiate. When have you demonstrated analytical skills when tackling a problem?

2. **Organisation/time management:** how do you organise yourself/manage your time? Do you keep a diary? Tell me about a time when you have had to juggle multiple commitments/demands. How did you prioritise tasks?

3. **Resilience:** tell me about a time when you have received negative feedback. How did the feedback affect you? What did you do after receiving the feedback? Tell me about a time when you have made a mistake.

4. **Communication skills:** discuss a time when you have given a presentation to a large audience. Do you have any networking experience?

5. **Teamwork:** discuss a time when you have worked in a team. How would you deal with a team member that is not pulling their weight? How do you ensure that your voice is heard in a group situation? Have you ever had to boost the morale of a group/team? If so, what strategies did you use?

6. **Leadership:** have you ever had to lead a team? If so, which challenges did you face and how did you deal with them?

7. **Drive and determination:** when have you demonstrated commitment in the face of adversity? Have you ever had to go above and beyond the call of duty to get things done? When have you excelled under pressure?

8. **Creativity/adaptability:** when have you had to think 'outside the box'? Have you ever had to demonstrate adaptability to meet expectations? When have you had to adapt yourself to deal/interact with a broad range of people?

9. **Openness to learning/developing:** what interests/hobbies are you engaged in outside of your studies? If you had the time and opportunity to learn a new skill, what would it be and why?

Common Ethical Questions

Firms may ask ethical questions in order to gain a greater insight into your character. They may alternatively simply want to see how you react under pressure and deal with difficult questions. There are not necessarily 'correct' answers to all ethical questions, but remember, professional ethics are absolute and firms want to ensure their employees act with integrity. Here are examples of the types of questions you may face (including some that I was personally asked during interviews).

Typical questions you may be asked:

1. When have you acted ethically? (have you volunteered/undertaken charity work?)

2. When have you done something ethically questionable?

3. Is it ever justifiable to lie?

4. Would you support a client's lie or mistake if to do otherwise would mean the firm loses the client?

5. Should your client pay a bribe if necessary to get the job done?

6. Would you ever pay a ransom?

Strengths-based Questions

Strengths-based questions in contrast involve firms assessing whether candidates' strengths align with the role for which they are applying. These types of questions are becoming increasingly popular with firms, so it is worth checking whether the firm to which you are applying takes this approach in interviews. Questions tend to centre upon how you behave in certain situations and/or how you spend your time, which in turn can provide firms with an insight into your character, your proficiencies and what you enjoy doing.

Evidence indicates that people who use their strengths more are happier, more confident, more engaged whilst working, more resilient and less stressed, more effective at developing themselves, more likely to perform well and achieve their goals and have high energy and self-esteem levels. You can read more about this at: www.cappeu.com/Portals/3/Files/Why_Strengths_The_Evidence.pdf.

Firms want to make sure not only that you are able to complete a task, but that such tasks make you tick. If your strengths align with the types of tasks you will likely be completing on a day-to-day basis, this could suggest that you are more likely to be energised by completing the tasks that you will be required to undertake.

This in turn may suggest you will enjoy the work to a greater extent and thus be more motivated to stay in the office and work long hours (if required) in order to ensure tasks are completed to the standard expected.

Conversely, if you have clearly learnt how to complete a particular task, but such tasks do not align with your strengths or energise you, this could suggest that regularly engaging in such work could tire you out and negatively affect your motivation and performance. Below are some examples of the types of questions you may be asked.

Typical questions you may be asked:

1. What are your strengths and weaknesses?

2. Which 3 qualities would you bring to this firm?

3. What motivates you?

4. What do you typically do during weekends?

5. What do you do to relax?

6. What is the biggest challenge you have faced?

7. When have you failed at something?

8. When have you been disappointed about something and how did you react?

9. When have you had to deal with a difficult situation whilst working in a team?

10. What stresses you out?

11. How would your friends describe you?

Your answers to the above questions can provide firms with an indication of your suitability to the role for which you are applying. Be prepared for potential rapid fire questioning on strengths. You could have to 50 questions in one interview!

- Your strengths and weaknesses could give a firm an indication of your ability to perform tasks that could be required of you in the future. Remember, everyone has weaknesses and you should never try to claim that you are the exception. Think about your weaknesses and how you have addressed them or found a way to work around them. Firms don't tend to like it where you try to categorise an obvious strength as a weakness and this can show a lack of self-awareness.

- Your motivations or indications of the ways in which you spend your free time could indicate to a firm whether you are likely to enjoy (and thus be energised by) the type of work you are likely to undertake.

- The ways in which your have dealt with and responded to challenges, failures or difficult situations could provide an insight into your ability to tackle complex work (of which there is a lot in the City!) or handle yourself during stressful periods. There is plenty of complex work and stress involved in working in the City!

- Your responses to questions about others' perceptions about you could provide an insight into your self-awareness.

- Your responses to ethical questions could demonstrate your integrity and pragmatism.

This is all relevant to the firm when assessing not just your capability to fulfil the role, but your overall *suitability* to the role. There is no point in lying when answering these questions. You can never be certain of the answer firms are expecting and moreover, if your honest answers truly indicate you would be unsuited to (and potentially miserable in) such a role, then it is probably best for both you and your employer if your application does not progress.

Perhaps have a think about which of your strengths align best with the firm and the role you are applying for and how to evidence these strengths in action during an interview. When answering strengths based questions, try linking your answers back not only to relevant experiences, but also to the skills you have developed and demonstrated whilst undertaking these experiences. You can access a free strengths-profile at www.jobmi.com.

Questions may alternatively focus on how successful you are at doing certain tasks, how often you complete such tasks and/or how you *feel* when completing certain tasks. Your answers to these questions may in turn provide the firm with an insight into how you are likely to respond and perform in the role for which you are applying.

Below are examples of the strengths and character insights firms may try to assess, and the types of behaviours and actions they may ask you about when doing so. Firms may ask you how you feel when (or how often you find yourself) demonstrating some of these behaviours and actions, or how successful you are when attempting to do so.

Drive and ambition

- Pushing yourself to get things done and succeed (even after setbacks).

- Working long hours to deliver work to a high quality and standard.

- Doing things which give you purpose.

Personal development

- Testing yourself in new, unfamiliar or difficult situations; seeking out new information; and learning from mistakes in order to nurture your personal growth and development.

- Taking responsibility and acting quickly and decisively, whilst remaining balanced and self-assured in difficult situations.

Interactions with others

- Learning from, motivating or competing against others.

- Explaining things to others in ways that are easy to understand.

- Make persuasive arguments for what you want people to do.

- Building a rapport and long-standing relationship with people quickly and easily.

- Listening intently to, helping and supporting others in difficult circumstances.

- Appreciating and valuing the role of others in your successes and giving credit to others when due.

Your attitude

- Maintaining a positive outlook even in difficult circumstances or making jokes/telling stories to lighten the mood.

- Standing up for what you believe in and upholding your values.

Your approach to work:

- Planning ahead and carefully organising well in advance.

- Focusing on the bigger picture and its implications/the opportunities available.

Type of work you find engaging

- Inventing something new, developing a different way of doing something or providing an alternate perspective.

- Spotting and rectifying mistakes and errors in pieces of work, or pre-empting issues that may arise and mitigating them in advance.

We have supplemented the above sections with a series of videos and articles relating to answering competency and strengths-based questions. These can be found at:

www.CityCareerSeries.com → Applications & Interviews → Competencies

The Careers Advisor's Perspective: How To Answer...

Claire Leslie, our friendly Careers Guru and acclaimed Careers Advisor, has helped thousands of students prepare for competency and strengths-based interviews. Here is some advice from Claire on how to tackle some of the trickier questions that come up.

How would your friends describe you?

You might be tempted to relax when facing this question. Perhaps the question conjures up the pleasing image of fun evenings with friends? Don't lose your focus. This isn't the time for the phrase "Party animal" to pop out. Thinking about the question in advance of an interview will ensure you are more able to give an impressive reply.

Why is the interviewer asking you the question?

The recruiter is trying to find out as much as possible about you. It's as important to know if you will fit into the existing teams, as it is to know if you can do the job. It's no good recruiting the excellent operator, who upsets everyone else in the workplace and causes all sorts of disruption. It's relevant to know what your friends think about you and indeed to know if you have friends!

The way in which you answer this question will give an insight into your self-awareness. How does what you say relate to the impression that the interviewer has formed about you in the interview? If you have come across as quiet and reserved and your answer is "fun and zany" then there is a mismatch. Why might that be? You may just have made the recruiter anxious.

What shouldn't you say?

This isn't the time to come out with a list of attributes you hope the interviewer wants to hear. You might be tempted to go with: "Oh, they think I am very bright and they know that I work really hard and that I am a complete perfectionist". It's not the best answer. This just doesn't sound as if it is the way friends talk about one another. You risk the interviewer deciding that you are being less than completely honest, which could be fatal.

Think about what picture your answer is going to give the interviewer. "Fun" gives the impression that you can make others laugh and make a social event go with a swing. The kind of person you might want in a workplace. "Party animal" might be another way of describing the same individual, but the picture it creates is different. I see the late night party, and then worry about the bleary eyed employee the following day.

What sort of words do friends use about one another?

Here are some of the words I would use about my friends: loyal, kind, always there for me, unselfish, funny, honest, practical (or sometimes impractical). The words I use refer to our emotional connection. Of course, many of my friends are also very clever, hard-working and good looking, but these are not the attributes which principally drive and maintain our friendship.

You may be thinking: surely the interviewer doesn't want to hear words like this? Well why not? Someone who can be described with some of the words I have used above is probably going to be a good team player, able to fit into the workplace. These are appropriate words which identify key reasons why people chose to be friends, so your answer is more likely to sound genuine and honest.

Why not do your research? Ask your friends how they would describe you. See if they are all saying the same thing; sometimes we can behave differently with different people. If the answers are different think about the real you. Come up with three words so that you are ready for this question. How to deliver the answer? Smile, you're talking about your friends - it makes me happy when I think about mine!

What was your greatest disappointment?

This type of question can give the interviewer an idea of how you handle adversity; the trouble is that you might not have had any significant adversity to deal with, or at least none that you want to share in an interview! So how are you going to answer?

What not to do?

You don't want to sound arrogant. Don't go for the wide-eyed look, accompanying an incredulous denial that you have ever been disappointed. This is unlikely to endear you to an interviewer, who probably has encountered one or two setbacks in his or her life.

This is not the time to bring up a genuine disaster. I certainly wouldn't recommend talking about one of life's great griefs like the loss of someone you loved. The emotions involved go far beyond any disappointment and you risk putting the interviewer in an embarrassing position or, worse, upsetting yourself and losing focus.

On the other hand you should avoid the utterly trivial. "I was disappointed when I burnt my dinner because I was looking forward to eating it" risks a laugh which could just be at you rather than with you! Use this approach only if you can't think of anything else and even then, only to buy yourself a bit more time. Start the laugh yourself. That way you can be sure that you're all laughing together and you might come across as the sort of person the interviewer would like to have in the office.

Dodging the question altogether is not really an option. The interviewer wants to know that you always learn from disappointment and change your behaviour accordingly. You might accumulate a negative comment on the interviewer's mark sheet if you fail to answer the question properly - definitely worth avoiding! Moreover, some interviewers simply will not let you move onto the next question until you have given an answer.

How can you find the happy compromise?

Start by thinking of an example which will allow you to showcase your resilience and your ability to overcome a problem. The exam which didn't go according to plan might work. You have probably already had to disclose your marks on an application form, so you won't be telling your prospective interviewer anything new. Did your disappointment make you reassess your work ethic, or take advice on how to improve?

Another option might be the disappointing decision you took for the greater good, but you'll have to be careful. It could be useful, for example, to talk about how you gave up an extracurricular activity to focus on your work and about the disappointment this caused you. You won't however want to imply that you do nothing but work!

You could also talk about the time you bowed to a majority decision which was at odds with what you wanted. You need to take care here too. If you ended up in this position, your powers of persuasion obviously didn't work! Do you need to be particularly persuasive for your preferred job?

It's also quite difficult to talk about what you learnt without potentially sounding petulant. How is the following comment going to go down?

"I did what everyone else wanted against my better judgement and it turned out badly. It proved that I was right all along".

If you are going to use this example, you'd be better saying:

"I went along with the majority and although I was initially disappointed it turned out fine. I learnt that it is important sometimes to be prepared to concede a point and that there can be advantages to doing this. It can give you a wholly new perspective on something."

Whatever you decide on this question, it definitely falls into the category of one you'll want to ponder in advance of the interview.

What is your greatest achievement?

The employer isn't looking for the marathon running, country representing, top-flight musician who has received an Oscar for acting and single-handedly solved the Greek debt crisis! Instead it is looking for the person who can demonstrate that he/she has done something other than just study. The answer can be equally impressive if you have worked alongside study to make ends meet, or spent a gap year persuading reluctant parents in Africa to allow their children to be inoculated against Polio.

Start very simply: "I think my greatest achievement is…/I am most proud of…" and then set out what you did. Use the STAR framework (explained earlier in this handbook). Describe the circumstances fairly briefly and then focus most of your answer on the action you took, but avoid hyperbole. Finish by reviewing the result and reflecting on the skills you gained. If your achievement was to work alongside study, then you'll have demonstrated a great work ethic, resilience and time management skills. If you have contributed to society, then you'll want to point out how your efforts have impacted individuals. If, however, following that amazing voluntary work you want to work in a profit-making City organisation, you might want to focus more on the skills you learnt. Communication? Teamwork? Persuasion and negotiation?

It's probably not a good idea to tell an investment bank that following your amazing experience working with the dispossessed, you have decided to work for the bank because you like its corporate social responsibility policy. Remember that the bank is "about" making money. Their staff need to buy into that idea. If they think that you just want to "help" they're probably going to wonder if you will be right for them.

Tell me about your cultural awareness

In this age of globalisation, cultural awareness is an overarching skill and a necessity. Demonstrating your flexibility, open-mindedness and your cultural awareness will always be important. During your time at university you are exposed to new experiences, including a range of different cultures and languages. These enriching learning experiences can be used in your working life. They develop you as a person and make you more employable; in the UK and in the wider world. Have you ever stopped to think about how culturally aware you are? Probably not. Few of us take the time to reflect on our skill sets or consider the gaps in them.

Why is the interviewer asking you the question?

Global companies will want to see that you are open to new ideas and cultures. Can you communicate with people from different nations and avoid any ambiguity? Can you build relationships that take account of different cultural expectations and needs? Do you always try to understand and value different perspectives whilst looking for the common ground? Will you be able to research new markets and cultures and have the sensitivity to check in with contacts when necessary to get clarification and iron out problems?

How can you demonstrate your cultural awareness?

Languages can be a great asset, but they are only one piece of a complex jigsaw. Networking at university with students from different nationalities can help to give you a better understanding of what is important in their countries. Researching specific markets and countries will give you a chance to identify trends in the global market whilst appreciating what each nation has to offer. You can also begin to understand the cultural values which sometimes lead to such confusion. Checking for clarification is vital and this is the hidden communication skill that is essential in a global marketplace. You've probably mixed with people from different cultures, faiths and even picked up the odd words of another language. Perhaps you are the person who has had the confidence to come to another country to learn another language, travel, study abroad or to build new networks. Start thinking about some examples. Reflect on how you have made the best of the multi cultural environment at university. Don't think that you won't need to worry about this if you are not aspiring to work for an international company. All recruiters want a broad range of skills to equip them to succeed in the global village.

Cultural awareness is about being open to embracing the diversity of life. It is about a willingness to learn and to seek new experiences and ultimately new friends. It is being open to what life and your career brings you. As you learn to understand more about the world, you'll find there is less certainty. Your cultural awareness will equip you to deal with the situations you and your employer faces. So what do you think you've learnt and how will you articulate it? What about talking about flexibility, resilience, accepting ambiguity (understanding there is no one right way) and interpersonal skills.

Where do you see yourself in 5 years' time?

When answering this (popular and tricky) interview question, most interviewees abandon any effort to be honest and simply provide the answer they think the interviewer would most like to hear. Is this the right tactic?

Why is the question being asked?

Interviewers ask you this question in the hope that your answer will demonstrate that your application has been carefully thought through, and that it will lead to a medium (if not long) term relationship between you and the employer. Below are some statistics to demonstrate why this is a legitimate concern for employers. Based on research involving almost 4000 employers (contained in the CEB Report – Driving New Success: Strategies in Graduate Recruitment 2014):

1.   1 in 4 graduates quit their first job within a year of starting work.

2.   66% of graduates say they regret their first job choice.

3.   The UK spend on graduate recruitment in 2013 was £888 million. It's estimated that £112 million of this was an investment which failed to yield a quality return.

How Should You Answer?

If you're convinced the job is right for you then you're probably at least half way to being able to give a compelling answer to the interview question. So, where do you start? Try asking yourself these questions… and then thinking about answers to them. This is the time for honest self-reflection, don't just think about what an employer wants to hear.

1.   Why did you apply for a job in this sector?

2.   What is it about this particular employer which is attractive?

3.   Why does the role appeal to you?

4.   What would a typical 5-year progression be? Is this what you want for yourself?

If you can't answer any of the above questions, then you probably haven't done enough research. Try looking at the details of the training offered and of the work you would be expected to undertake. What are people typically doing in 5 years' time? Is this where you want to be?

You could say that you hope to have settled in a department that you find particularly interesting and that you are adding value to whichever department you are in. Also, show that you understand how this employer is different from competitors. It is the time to be enthusiastic and to smile! Be positive but you don't have to be specific about the precise role you hope to be in; it's too early to know.

What If You Cannot Think Of An Answer?

You've prepared properly for the interview, it's all going swimmingly and then along comes a tricky question … suddenly your mind goes completely blank. It's happened to us all, but what you do next might determine whether it's game over, or whether you can prove your resilience and get a bit closer to that job offer.

The first thing you need to do is think about what kind of question you are facing. This will determine your response.

A competency question

I once froze at interview when I was asked to talk about a time when I had worked with someone difficult. Now, I have, over the years, worked with plenty of difficult people, so why did I suddenly forget? Probably because I hadn't seen this coming – poor planning – and because what sprang into my mind was a negative experience. I did not want to talk about this at interview. It is never good to be negative about previous employment.

I did the right thing, I asked to come back to the question later, but then I let it play on my mind while I answered successive questions. It distracted me and impacted my performance. Do ask to come back to a question but don't then stop concentrating on everything else! As mentioned earlier in this handbook, listing out and carefully considering all the experiences you have accumulated in advance can help you to think up examples on the spot when unexpected questions come up.

A technical question

If your degree is relevant to the role for which you are applying, then you might find that you are asked technical questions. Try not to panic about questions you find difficult; the more anxious you are, the more likely it is that your mind will go blank. Take time to think. Employers will almost always be happy for you to pause; they would rather have an employee who reflects on difficult questions than one who rushes in and makes errors!

Remember that a pause while you think will feel much longer to you than it actually is. Also remember that employers may ask questions knowing that you will likely be unable to answer them. They may simply be looking to test: (a) how well you react under pressure; (b) how well you can apply logic on the spot to reach a reasonable conclusion; and (c) the point at which you no longer have an answer (i.e. where your knowledge ends)! You might have got a lot further than other candidates before you had to admit defeat, even though it may not feel like this at the time. Try not to feel deflated or let your disappointment at not answering everything play on your mind during the rest of the interview.

An oddball question

Oddball (i.e. unexpected and seemingly random) questions are often talked about and feared. How many bricks are there in Birmingham? How many pints of milk are drunk each day in the UK? You are not expected to know the answer to these questions, just try not to freeze completely. The important thing is how you start to think and reason your way to an answer. Demonstrate that you are logical and can keep calm under pressure and you are already on the road to success. The City Career Series Consultancy Handbook explains how to answer such "brainteaser" and "market sizing" questions in more detail.

A strengths-based question

You would have thought that a question about how you spend your spare time or what you do to relax would be very simple. However, sometimes these questions can floor you. You may be trying to think of something which *you believe* sounds worthwhile and impressive, when actually in truth you like going shopping with friends! It's worth thinking about answers in advance (using the 'Strengths-based Questions' section of this handbook for guidance), and ensure that you have a really clear understanding of the skills an employer is looking. Ultimately, if the unexpected question comes up, you need to answer honestly. You're likely to get caught out in a strengths-based interview if you lie.

A commercial awareness question

Everyone knows that you need to exhibit an understanding of the business world if you want to land that graduate job. Generally you will be able to choose what news item you want to talk about, but what if you get asked a totally unexpected question? How about, "What companies would you invest in if you had £1 million?". This sort of question demands the knack of applying the knowledge you have, and the ability to keep calm and to start talking logically. It's about buying yourself some time while you wait for inspiration to strike. Perhaps in this context you might start by considering broader sector areas (e.g. oil, pharmaceuticals, property) or businesses in emerging markets. Obviously to pull this off, you must have kept up with the news.

So the lessons to take from all this? There will be times in an interview when no answer springs to mind. Prepare as comprehensively as possible in advance. Treat interviews a bit like exams – the more you prepare, the less likely it is that you will face a question that you do not know how to answer. Generally try to keep calm, take a deep breath and don't be afraid to ask for thinking time or clarification.

For career-related guidance and comprehensive advice relating to a wide range of application and interview questions, you should check out Claire's fantastic YouTube channel:

youtube.com/universityofwarwickstudentcareersskills

The Recruiter's Perspective

In this section of the handbook, recruiters from top City firms have provided exclusive advice to help you succeed.

Key competencies required to succeed in the City (Freshfields)

This isn't an exhaustive list of the qualities we want to see and every firm will be looking for something slightly different. However, demonstrating these attributes effectively will help to set you apart!

Analytical ability

This is at the heart of what it means to be an effective solicitor. But what do recruiters really mean by this? Well, it's the ability to identify key issues, to explain concepts clearly, to think laterally, to argue and defend a point effectively, and to see both the big picture and the detail. Difficult to demonstrate on an application form? Not really – the Freshfields application form (with its 850-word personal statement) tests not only the content of your statement but also how it's assembled. Does your approach show a clear, logical mind? Are your reasons for commercial law not only convincing but also well put together? Are you not just smart, but smart in your delivery?

Commercial interest

At Freshfields, what we are really testing for is commercial interest, rather than simply commercial knowledge or commercial awareness. The latter may come from 10 minutes spent hurriedly with *The FT* before an interview. Commercial interest derives from a genuine curiosity about the commercial world around you – and we think that interest is difficult to fake. Have you ever thought about the way that organisations work and the concerns they have? Who runs them and for whose benefit? How their activities are financed? How they measure success and failure? What constraints there are on their growth? Who, if anyone, regulates them? That's commercial interest.

Interpersonal skills

Our recruits must be sensitive to those around them, able to relate to different people well, to form good relationships with clients and adapt well to the firm's ethos. So we are looking at your body language and eye contact. How do you describe your relations with others? How have you dealt with a difficult personal issue or what annoys you about other people? Through the (understandable!) interview nerves, can we see you developing the necessary self-confidence to win the trust of clients and colleagues? And, crucially, do you have a good sense of humour?

Determination and drive

We need people who can cope with the pace of life at Freshfields and the demands made of them by partners, clients and commercial life. We need highly motivated people who will be able and willing to devote energy to their roles and cope with a variety of demands on different jobs with flexibility and commitment. So we want to know how much you pack into your life, how proactive you are (do you lead or take the initiative, or do you just turn up?) and how you overcome difficulties. What do you get out of your studies and activities? What are you looking for in a job and what energises you?

Organisation and discipline

Freshfields lawyers must be organised in their approach to the massive deals and cases on which they will work; they need to be sure they have checked all relevant sources of information and that nothing is left to chance. So we are interested in how you organise your time. How do you prioritise between different activities? How do you know when you've done enough? We need to know that you can multi-task and that you can keep your cool.

Team playing

This is not just about playing in teams or working in committees. We need people who are interested in the common good and not personal glory – who may be leaders, but who will look after the interests of other team players, too. To what extent do you use 'I' as opposed to 'we'? Are you good at taking instructions and receiving feedback? Have you shown that you can get on with a range of people from different backgrounds?

For more information on Freshfields, please visit the below websites:

www.freshfields.com/ukgraduates

Twitter @freshfieldsgrad

Facebook @ FreshfieldsGraduates

Instagram @ freshfieldsgrads

When have you undertaken a leadership role? (Ashurst)

Tell us about a time where you have undertaken a leadership role and outline the skills you used in this position

Employers want to know which skills you believe are most important for the role. This will help to show your understanding of the role and of what the firm is looking for from applicants. For almost any role in the City, leadership and teamwork are very important skills, so you must be able to demonstrate that you have developed these skills when answering application and interview questions. Leadership and teamwork are key skill sets that are somewhat intertwined. You can expect questions centering on these skills to come up time and time again when tackling application and interview questions for almost any role.

Teamwork vs. Leadership

Being a team player is key to building and maintaining relationships – within your team, with your wider colleagues or with clients. This is why we need to know that you understand the importance of working in a team to achieve a shared goal, even as a leader, and that you have the ability to do so.

Being an effective leader is key to motivating others to work efficiently and effectively and ensuring projects are completed on time, to the standards expected. While you may not immediately be taking a leadership role if you are offered the position for which you are applying, the interviewer needs to know that once your career progresses, you will be able to effectively lead others as your responsibility increases. This is why we ask about your leadership experiences/qualities.

How to prepare and deliver your answer

It is good practice to think of some examples of when you have worked in a team and when you have undertaken a leadership role. Have these examples at the forefront of your mind and be prepared to discuss them in detail. It is important that your examples are relevant, that you have more than one example ready for both skillsets, and that you do not prepare generic "model" answers – you cannot anticipate the exact phrasing of a question in advance and your prepared answer may not quite answer it. On this note, it is important to listen to the precise question the interviewer is asking, as answering a slightly different question could make your answer seem less genuine and may reflect less favourably on your communication skills.

This question can be answered in numerous different ways as leadership roles can take many forms. A good answer will include enough detail about the role and what exactly it entailed. Were you elected into the leadership position? What did your role in particular involve? What did your team set out to achieve and how tight was the deadline? Did you face any challenges? If so, how did you resolve these problems? This is a particularly popular angle for employers to take, as it helps us to examine your self-awareness and test your ability to succeed under pressure and overcome challenges.

It is important to distinguish between using the words 'I' and 'we', as we want to know about your responsibilities, albeit in the context of the wider team. A good candidate will explain how they distributed certain tasks and responsibilities to their wider team, demonstrating that they knew which tasks were appropriate to delegate and that they played to the strengths of their individual team members to achieve the overarching goal.

This article was written by the graduate recruitment team at Ashurst (an international law firm), exclusively for City Career Series. For more information on Ashurst, please visit the below websites or contact the graduate recruitment team at gradrec@ashurst.com.

careers.ashurst.com
www.ashurst.com
www.facebook.com/AshurstTrainees

What is "commercial awareness" and why is it important? (Allen & Overy)

What is commercial awareness?

This is a question that we ask to test whether candidates truly understand the type of work undertaken by commercial lawyers and what this could mean for them in the future. We expect students to identify that 'commercial awareness' is having an understanding of the context in which City firms operate. It is an awareness of the economic and business landscape that helps businesses and individuals to understand their clients, their businesses, their priorities, their competitors, and relevant industry sectors. This ensures they can offer informed, contextual advice to whoever requires it.

Commercial awareness is not just restricted to the consideration of legal issues; it can enable you to anticipate the impact of the economic climate, political environment, current affairs, and market trends and developments in order to maximise a client's opportunities and minimise their exposure to risk.

Why is commercial awareness important for City workers?

A&O Graduate Recruitment Partner Claire Wright explains that 'fundamentally, a lawyer is not just a practitioner of law but also a business advisor. You will be dealing with complex business transactions covering multiple jurisdictions at A&O and we need to know that our lawyers are able to offer practical and innovative advice and solutions to large, global corporates, financial institutions, regulators and governments. The legal, economic and technology landscape is constantly changing and so there is more pressure than ever in a competitive market for us to be able to offer our clients the very best commercial legal advice.'

Why is commercial awareness important for applicants?

The legal landscape is constantly shifting and changing, bringing with it new challenges and opportunities every day. Commercially aware applicants challenge the status quo and consider the commercial context, helping them to adapt quickly and provide informed, expert legal advice that is commercially viable.

'An ability to demonstrate good commercial awareness is what sets a candidate apart from their peers' says Hannah Rolph, Graduate Recruitment and LL.M Specialist at Allen & Overy. 'The best lawyers are the ones that show a genuine interest in what is going on in both the legal and business worlds. They have a better understanding of commercial issues, and can think practically about how key decisions will affect their firm and its clients. That is why we focus so intently on evaluating our applicants' understanding of wider business issues.'

Jake Schogger, former A&O Summer Vacation Scheme attendee (and the author of this book) explains that commercial awareness provided him with essential context that enabled him to better understand interview case studies and the transactions to which he was exposed during his vacation scheme. He was consequently able to participate in informed discussions with interviewers and supervisors, which demonstrated his enthusiasm in respect of the work the firm carries out and his willingness to learn. This in turn was positively reflected in his feedback.

Recent Associate Luke Sampson adds that 'in interviews, employers are looking for far more than an aptitude for law; I found that a basic awareness of how companies operate, the nature and range of financial products, and the function of the global markets helped me to demonstrate an understanding of transactional and advisory legal work in its wider commercial context – having not done a law degree, I felt that was really important.'

This article was written by the Graduate Recruitment team at Allen & Overy (an international law firm), exclusively for City Career Series. For more information on graduate and undergraduate opportunities at Allen & Overy, please visit the below websites or contact the graduate recruitment team at graduate.recruitment@allenovery.com.

www.aograduate.com
www.facebook.com/allenoverygrads
@AllenOveryGrads
Snapchat: AllenOveryGrads.

ALLEN & OVERY

Career Motivation

Many candidates struggle to articulate their motivation for pursuing a particular career. However, this can be an incredibly important aspect of interviews and you should give this element some serious thought when preparing. This question will typically come up during competency interviews, although some firms may have specific interviews dedicated to a candidate's motivation for applying for a particular role.

Tell the story of how your interest in your chosen career has developed. For instance, when and why did your interest in your chosen career first materialise? Was it at school whilst studying a particular subject, whilst undertaking work experience, or following a conversation with an acquaintance working in that industry? What did you do to further explore this interest (e.g. undertake certain work experience)? How did your research confirm that this was the right career for you? Ensure your answer is sensible however. Stating that you have always wanted to be a lawyer/banker/consultant/accountant/actuary etc. may not come across as genuine and believable to your interviewer!

Below are some of the aspects that you may want to keep in mind when considering your personal reasons for pursuing your chosen career. However, *do not* just parrot these justifications to interviewers. Remember, many firms will have seen this handbook and may think you are merely reciting phrases from it as opposed to relaying your genuine personal motivations. Furthermore, your answers will be unconvincing unless you relate them back to your own personal experiences.

Career aligns with your interests

- Does the work conducted by the firm/division to which you are applying align with your personal interests? If so, explain what initially made you want to work in a commercial domain and how you then pursued this interest and discovered that commercial law/banking/audit/consultancy (etc.) was the career for you.

- Have you particularly enjoyed studying school subjects or university modules (e.g. Economics, Business, Finance, or commercially-oriented Law modules such as Contract) that relate to your chosen career? Have you undertaken relevant work experiences that you found especially interesting? If so, *why*? Have you enjoyed certain elements of your studies or extracurricular activities that you believe will form an integral part of your chosen career, for instance researching, problem solving, working in a team, or presenting?

- Discussing other careers that you have considered can help to validate your answers. If you have undertaken internships at other types of professional services firms, mention the elements of these careers that you did not like so much and explain the elements of your chosen career that appeal to you more. For instance, if you decide you want to be a commercial lawyer but have previously undertaken an investment banking internship, explain what you liked less about investment banking (perhaps the focus on numbers?) and then explain the elements of a career in commercial law that appeal to a greater extent (perhaps the focus on language?).

Intellectual Fulfilment & Working Environment

- What is it about the nature of the work that appeals? Does the firm engage in unique, interesting work that is likely to provide a constant intellectual challenge? Does a pressurised, dynamic working environment appeal? Are you interested in working with high profile-clients on headline-grabbing deals? Does the prospect of regularly working in a team appeal? If a career appeals for any of these reasons then explain *why* this is the case.

- Do these elements suggest a career will remain dynamic, varied and stimulating? Perhaps this indicates you will rarely find yourself clock-watching or feeling unfulfilled? Support your statements by providing personal examples to illustrate that certain aspects of the career *genuinely* appeal. Have you particularly enjoyed working in a similar working environment (e.g. spending long hours undertaking challenging work) in the past when engaging in group projects or work experience? Have you enjoyed participating in workshops designed to simulate the type of work in which the firm engages? If you have not accumulated such experiences, have you experienced the opposite type of working environment? Did this make you realise that you would prefer to work in a more pressurised or dynamic environment?

- I had taken on a variety of jobs throughout my education, including a paper round, a job pushing trolleys in a supermarket and a job lifting wooden planks up staircases on a building site. I compared these experiences to my chosen career, explaining that although my previous jobs typically involved favourable working hours and little stress, I had not felt intellectually engaged and felt that I had lacked the opportunity to significantly develop my personal skills and capabilities. This meant that I lacked a sense of personal fulfilment and achievement, which is why I wanted instead to pursue an intellectually challenging career and work in a dynamic and pressurised working environment.

People & Culture

- Does the prospect of working with bright, ambitious, like-minded people on a daily basis appeal? If so, *why*? Will this provide you with significant opportunities to learn and develop? Does this also appeal on a social level?

- If you discuss the people however, be ready to explain how you have come to realise that the people are of a certain calibre and character. Was it during office visits or networking events that you interacted with City workers and gained this impression? If you have met people from the firm at which you are interviewing, perhaps mention them by name and outline your interactions.

International Element

- If you are interviewing at an international firm, explain why the international element of the career appeals. How can you demonstrate your desire to work on international transactions? Have you chosen to study abroad, attended international study programmes, travelled extensively or elected to learn multiple languages?

- If not, do you simply feel that the opportunity to engage in complex, cross-border transactions will provide the greatest possible intellectual challenge? Does the prospect of working with other employees and clients from a variety of countries and cultures indicate your career will remain interesting and varied? To substantiate such a claim, you could relay any positive past experiences you may have of working in a team with people from a variety of different backgrounds.

Training & Development

- What is it about the training offered by firms in your chosen industry that particularly appeals? Do firms in that industry focus more on the personal development of candidates and/or provide variety unmatched by other professions?

- As mentioned, do not just recite the phrases in this handbook. This will not necessarily come across as convincing. Support your statements. Give examples of when you have enjoyed experiencing a particularly steep learning curve in the past, or discuss the conversations you have had with workers in that industry about their positive training experiences.

Typical questions you may be asked:

1. What influenced your decision to pursue this particular career?

2. Which other professions have you considered and why did you not want to pursue them instead?

3. If you had to work in any other industry, which would you choose and why?

4. What is your understanding of the role for which you are applying?

5. Where do you see yourself in 10 years' time?

We have supplemented the above section with a series of videos and articles relating to career motivation questions. These can be found at:

www.CityCareerSeries.com → Applications & Interviews → Motivation Questions

Firm Motivation & Research

Graduate recruiters will expect you to have thought carefully about *why* you want to work at their firm. There will be more candidates capable of carrying out the work at the level required than the number of available places. Firms will not hire people who cannot demonstrate a genuine interest in working at that firm in particular. Hiring a student to undertake an internship is a fairly substantial investment for a firm to make. Consider the cost of paying interns, the value of partner/director and associate hours required to accommodate, train and assess interns, the expense of arranging social events etc.

If you receive two or three rejections for answering 'why this firm?' too generically, odds are you would receive another fifty rejections if you simply tried to hedge your bets through applying to more firms. This is one of the reasons why you tend see candidates receiving either no offers or multiple offers. By all means apply to 10 or 11 firms, but only if you have the time to undertake sufficient research in order to ensure your answers are not too generic.

You may well be asked which other firms you have applied to so be prepared to justify these choices and why the present firm is your first choice. It is fine to apply to a range of firms for work experience/internships in order to gain a balanced insight into the different options available. However, if all your choices combined suggest you have no idea about the *type* of firm in which you are interested or have no particular interest in the type of work in which the present firm engages, this may suggest you are unsure of what you are actually looking for (in turn suggesting you are a risky choice for the firm to make).

Do not give generic reasons for applying to that firm that merely reflect a quick skim of the firm's marketing materials. Think of legitimate ways to differentiate the firm and more importantly, relate these elements back to *you* in order to convince recruiters that these factors genuinely appeal. Which of your personal experiences have made the firm's culture, values, reputation and training structure appeal to you? Here are some potential factors you could consider when preparing your application and interview answers.

Reputation, Work, Sectors & Clients

- It is ok to mention that you are attracted to the firm as a result of its reputation. However, you must explain *why* this is the case, linking your answer back to *you*.

- Do you like the range and quality of clients that the firm attracts? Does this indicate a career at the firm will remain varied and stimulating? If you mention that you like the fact that the work is high profile, then what distinguishes the firm from its direct competitors? Have they won certain awards or engaged in unique and/or groundbreaking deals?

- Does the firm have a sector focus or market-leading capability that particularly appeals? Do you have a particular interest in that sector/capability? If so, explain *why* these elements particularly appeal to you.

Growth

- Has the firm demonstrated a desire to progress and grow? Have new offices been opened in jurisdictions not yet explored by competitors? Why does this appeal? Is the firm excelling in a region that particularly takes your interest?

- If the firm has been involved in a high profile acquisition, know the details. Why did they proceed with the acquisition? Was it successful? How could this affect the firm's future?

- If the firm is truly international, why does this appeal? Perhaps you would like the opportunity to work for a firm with a global network of offices as this could provide the greatest potential to receive support and benefit from expertise relating to a wider-variety of issues?

- It can be advisable to avoid talking about the firm as if it is a travel agency however! Travel opportunities vary between firms and industries and thus focusing on your desire to travel may present you as an unsuitable candidate for a particular role. An international network of offices does not automatically mean the firm will be looking to offer extensive travel opportunities to its employees, especially at the more junior levels.

People, Culture & Values

- The easiest way to differentiate some firms (many of which engage in a similar level of work for similar clients) is through considering its people and culture. If you have spoken to employees at campus presentations, networking dinners or office visits, mention why you liked them and how this impacted upon your perception of the firm. Do not be afraid to mention their names, as retaining such information can demonstrate your genuine interest in the firm.

- Does it seem that the culture is welcoming, supportive and non-hierarchal? Does the firm put a higher focus on volunteering and social opportunities for its employees than others? If so, why does this appeal to you? Do you feel you are most likely to succeed in a non-hierarchal working environment? Have you spent a lot of your free time volunteering and is this something you would like to continue to do? However, whilst volunteering is something that may be worth mentioning, do not focus *too* much on it.

Past Experience

- Have you visited the firm before? If so, what did you like about it? If you got involved in any work, be prepared to talk about this in detail.

Training & Development

- What is it about the training offered by the firm that particularly appeals? Does the training on offer suggest that the firm really focuses on the personal development of its employees and provides variety unmatched by other firms?

- Do opportunities exist to experience a variety of different departments? Do you have unrivalled opportunities to work in overseas offices? Is the training uniquely structured (for instance, 3 month rotation opportunities)?

- What kind of supervision and support are you provided throughout? Do you have dedicated mentors or frequent appraisals? Are there focused training sessions and/or seminars on offer? Are external speakers invited to talk or is there an academy you are able to attend?

- Does the size of the intake appeal? Does this suggest you will receive greater responsibility during the early stages of your career? Is the firm highly ranked across a range of departments (which in turn perhaps suggests you will receive high quality training if your training involves rotation between different departments)? Are you afforded an opportunity to further develop your skill sets (e.g. are grants available for language courses)? Is further education encouraged? Does the firm offer unique opportunities for further study, for instance funded MBAs? Do you have the opportunity to spend some time abroad (as is the case with some US-headquartered firms)?

Research

- You can access information on firms through a number of sources. You could start with the firm's website, its annual review, articles it has published and its profile on other websites. Follow the firm on Twitter, LinkedIn and Facebook and keep up to date with firm news relating to deals, poignant developments, awards and expansion plans. Sources such as The Lawyer (Law candidates), the Financial Times and the Economist can also be useful.

- However (and this cannot be reiterated enough!), be wary of regurgitating this information without explaining why certain aspects of the firm particularly appeal to you. It is likely that the graduate recruitment team wrote at least some of the content on these research sources and thus simply reproducing the information found could give the impression that your research was shallow.

- Speaking to firm employees during campus presentations, career fairs and open days could give you a better insight into a firm's culture and the day-to-day life of an employee. This information may be less accessible to other candidates and could thus help to set you apart in interviews. Take notes! You may not interview at that firm for another year and a half and will thus be unlikely to remember everything you are told. Also, use your network. If there are students at your university that have already interned at the firm, or friends, family (even lecturers) that have previously worked for the firm, approach them and question them on their personal experiences.

Typical questions you may be asked:

1. Why do you want to work for this firm?

2. Which other firms have you applied to and why do you prefer this firm?

3. Talk about a particular deal the firm has been involved in and why you found it interesting.

4. If you took over the firm today, what would you do? You could answer this based on the following two questions…

5. What are the major challenges facing this firm?

6. Where would you next open an office and which office would you close?

We have supplemented the above section with a series of videos and articles relating to firm motivation questions. These can be found at:

www.CityCareerSeries.com → Applications & Interviews → Motivation Questions

Current Affairs & Industries

In a majority of interviews, I was (at least to some extent) able to lead the direction of the interview when discussing current affairs. I was not asked random questions about issues I knew nothing about, but instead was either asked to talk about something that I had recently read in the news or something relating to another statement I had made. For instance, if I mentioned a firm's expertise in Project Finance, I may then have been asked to discuss one of the firm's Project Finance transactions.

If you mention a deal or discuss a current issue in your application, this could come up during your interview. Commercial awareness is very important in this context. City workers are generally expected to have at least a basic awareness and understanding of the most topical issues affecting their client's business and industry. They need to ensure that any proposal made or advice given is informed and contextualised.

What to consider when reading the news

- When discussing your chosen (or delegated) topic, you must not only explain the topic/issue itself, but more importantly, how this relates to both the firm and its clients and what your opinion is (including an assessment of the counter opinion). Below are some basic examples to provide some indication of the considerations you could take into account.

- If you are discussing newly implemented regulation relating to the investment activities of banks or the ability of corporations to minimise their tax liabilities, consider whether this could impede the ability of those affected by the regulation to maintain or exceed previous profitability levels? If banks are more restricted in their ability to invest or corporations face higher tax bills, could this indicate their profit levels will reduce? Could this in turn indicate that they may be unable to continuing investing (for instance purchasing other companies or assets) to the same extent in the future? How would this affect the firm? Could it result in a reduction in the amount of M&A work that the firm receives? Conversely, could new regulation provide any opportunities for the firm? For instance, clients could require legal assistance to help them to understand (and thus ensure compliance with) the new legislation, or clients may require the firm to train its employees to ensure compliance internally.

- If there is an oil crisis and some of the firms' major clients are oil companies, how will this affect the clients' performances? How will this affect the firm's work flow? How might the firm be able to help out? How could the firm hedge its position by pursuing other opportunities or industries?

- If you are discussing a weakened economy or an influx of insolvencies in the context of a commercial law interview, could this provide any opportunities for the firm's Insolvency practice (if it has one)? Could there be a general increase in disputes as companies sue each other to recover payments owed in the fear that their debtors will otherwise become insolvent and thus default on the debt? Is the firm's Litigation practice well placed to win this type of work from its clients?

Topics

- If there is a particular topic that is consistently discussed on the front pages prior to your interview (for instance, regulation, tax avoidance, political instability, elections, disasters, emerging markets, whether Scotland should become independent, whether England should remain in the EU etc.), then try to gain some insight into the topic before the interview. There is every chance the interviewer will bring it up.

- In addition, check the front page of the Financial Times on the morning of your interview just in case something major has happened. I would have been caught out had I not checked the Financial Times on the morning of my very first interview. A major change had been announced relating to the primary topic (which incidentally related to banking regulation) that I had prepared to discuss in the interview.

- The interviewer of course brought up this change as soon as discussions relating to that topic began. Had I not known what the interviewer was talking about, who knows whether an internship offer would have been made as it may have come across as though I had only a superficial interest in current affairs.

- A topic that comes up fairly often in some way or another is the challenges facing the industry to which you are applying. You may for instance be asked what challenges the firm is facing, or what you would do if you took over the firm today. Understanding some potential challenges could provide some essential context when answering such questions. Clients are increasingly looking for greater value for money. The financial services industry in certain jurisdictions is heavily saturated. How does this affect firms from a business perspective? Is it becoming harder to compete? How can these issues be mitigated? Should further expansion into less saturated markets be pursued? If so, should a new office be opened (and where), or should the firms collaborate with local firms abroad? Should firms develop innovative ways to provide additional value to clients? Remember, different firms will experience different challenges depending on their size, sector-focus and specialisms, so do not prepare generic answers to be used across the board.

Firm & Industry Analysis

- When reading about a firm (e.g. the firm you are applying to or one of its clients), a particular issue (e.g. an upcoming general election) or a particular proposal (e.g. should England leave the EU?), you could use a SWOT and/or PESTLE analysis framework to ensure that your application/interview answers are clearly and logically structured.

- A SWOT analysis can be used to conduct an internal review of how a business is performing and how well it is positioned to take advantage of present/future opportunities and tackle any present/future challenges. It involves assessing the Strengths and Weaknesses of a business, alongside the Opportunities and Threats that have arisen/may arise by virtue of the market(s) in which it operates.

- A PESTLE analysis can be used to conduct a review of the external environment in which a business operates. The Political, Economic, Sociological, Technological, Legal and Environmental factors affecting a business' industry/market are considered. Frameworks such as these can prove useful in helping you to structure your answers coherently and can help you to develop your ability to think critically and to breakdown, analyse and structure salient points derived from large amounts of information. This ability can be incredibly important in the context of delivering presentations or liaising with clients!

We have produced a series of articles analysing a variety of different industries. These can be found at:

www.CityCareerSeries.com → Commercial Awareness → Industry Analyses

How to develop your knowledge and understanding of current affairs

- There are many other sources you can use to build your awareness, knowledge and understanding of current affairs. BBC Business News (online) provides a concise and straightforward account of current affairs. Helpfully, there are usually links at the bottom of articles to related articles. Reading these can help you to build a more comprehensive understanding of different topics. The Financial Times and the Economist (both in print and online) similarly provide an overview of the most relevant topical issues affecting the business and finance world. Some sources let you subscribe to useful 'daily digest' summaries of key news articles, which can really help to keep you abreast of what is going on in the business world. Consider following well-known commentators and publications on Twitter, delving into blogs focusing on financial services, reading client alerts published by firms and searching out YouTube videos focusing on particular topical issues.

- If a particular issue has attracted widespread debate (for instance, whether the UK should leave the EU), look for supplementary articles or journals exploring the wider issues surrounding the story (this is something I did when exploring articles on corporate tax avoidance for instance). Interviewers may want to see whether you can provide a balanced, critical opinion on the topic (including acknowledgement of the pros and cons where relevant).

- A technique that can work well involves copying and pasting major headlines from news websites into a Word document. When additional stories are published detailing developments on the issues captured in these headlines, paste these stories underneath the original headlines, thus creating a more substantial insight into topical events and issues. This can really help you to boost your general knowledge and understanding of what is going on in the world and to keep track of developments in the news.

- Try to place an additional focus on two to three topical issues that really engage and interest you. Research into them in greater depth and consider not only the debate and critical analysis surrounding the issues, but also the ways in which the issues could affect City firms and their clients. I created mini reports, which really helped to enhance my knowledge and understanding of those topical issues.

- In taking such an approach, you will essentially be building your own personal archive of the stories that (1) most interest you and (2) are currently topical. On interview days, you will therefore have a document that you can quickly and conveniently refer back to in order to remind yourself of the news stories that you have followed.

Typical questions you may be asked:

1. What have you read about in the news recently?

2. How does this particular news article relate to the firm and its clients?

3. What are the major challenges facing the industry that you intend to work in?

4. What is your opinion on [topical news story]?

5. If you could make one change in the law, what would it be?

6. In the next 12 to 18 months, which industry developments do you feel will have the greatest impact?

7. If you received £1 million, how would you invest it?

We have supplemented the above section with a series of videos and articles relating to current affairs. These can be found at:

www.CityCareerSeries.com → Commercial Awareness → Topical Current Affairs

Other Application Questions

'Prizes, Awards & Achievements' or 'Additional Information' Boxes

Many application forms tend to have a box in which candidates can include any additional information or an explanation of the prizes, awards and achievements they have accumulated. Candidates are typically unsure of which information should go into this box instead of being used as part of their answers to other questions.

You can include not only prizes and awards you that have received, but other achievements.

- Did you receive the top grades at your school or place in the top percentile in Europe/worldwide for a particular subject (even if you did not receive a 'prize' as such for doing so)? Were you asked to be Head Boy/Girl or a Prefect at school? Have you received any bursaries or scholarships?

- Have you reached a particular sporting, dance, drama or musical instrument grade/level? Have you won any competitions (be it horse riding or mooting, go kart racing or a virtual stock market challenge)? Have you successfully completed a (half) marathon or climbed a mountain?

- Are you experienced using particular software or technology (e.g. WestLaw, Microsoft Office or Bloomberg terminals)?

- Alternatively, have you managed to keep up to speed with your degree despite having to work part-time in order to fund yourself?

Consider whether certain achievements may have occurred too far into the past to reflect on your current character and abilities. Perhaps only include prizes and achievements that occurred several years ago if they are particularly pertinent.

Other Interview Questions

Icebreaker Questions

Some interview questions may not fall neatly within the aforementioned categories. Instead, they may be used as icebreakers or to provide an insight into your thought processes. Below are some examples of questions that you may be asked. Think about these too before an interview.

Typical questions you may be asked:

1. What made you choose your degree?

2. What made you want to study in England (if you are an international student)?

3. What influenced your decision to do a Masters degree?

4. How did you research which degree/university to choose?

5. What would your friends say about you?

Online Tests

Psychometric tests, situational judgement tests and E-tray exercises are used by firms to test certain skills and abilities that applications and interviews may be less effective at assessing. Tests can also be used by firms to whittle down the vast number of applicants to a more manageable pool of interviewees.

Although candidates are usually required to complete these tests online from a place of their choosing, some firms may require candidates to complete tests as part of assessment centres in those firms' offices (and these tests may not be computerised). Many firms simply require candidates to meet a certain fixed benchmark in order to progress through this stage of the interview process (although most refuse to reveal what that benchmark is).

Psychometric tests are to a large extent intuitive and different methods of tackling them better suit different people. It is thus difficult in this brief handbook to provide extensive guidance. However, I will provide a brief insight into some of the tests that are commonly encountered and offer some tips and techniques that I personally found to be of help when completing numerous tests throughout my time at university.

Types Of Test

The most commonly found tests are: (1) verbal reasoning tests); (2) logical reasoning tests (typically SHL); (3) numerical reasoning tests (typically SHL and usually not set by law firms); (4) situational judgement tests (typically tailored to the specific firm to which you are applying); and (5) E-Tray or email simulation exercises.

Most tests are in a multiple choice format and require you to select only one answer, although some firms use tests that are specifically tailored to them or tests produced by different organisations. This section of the handbook will focus only on the most commonly found psychometric tests (namely those produced by SHL and the Watson Glaser test). Some tests may involve negative marking, in which case guessing answers may not be advisable. It may be worth checking whether this is the case before taking a particular test.

General Tips

All the tests put you under time pressure, so you must strictly pace yourself. Find out how long you have to complete the test and how many questions you will face, then work out the time you have to answer each question and monitor the clock!

Some tests (e.g. SHL tests) do not let you scroll back and change answers once you have confirmed your choice, whereas others (e.g. Watson Glaser tests) let you move between answers as much as you like until your time runs out. Do not linger for too long on one particular question as you may as a result miss out on the opportunity to answer questions later on for which you do know the answer. With tests that let you scroll backwards and forwards between questions, try making a note of each question that you are unsure about on a piece of paper and then move swiftly onto to the next question so that you have a greater opportunity to respond to questions that you know the answer to. Return to the questions you were unsure about if you have time at the end.

Verbal Reasoning Tests

Format

Firms typically use SHL or Watson Glaser verbal reasoning tests. Verbal reasoning tests usually involve clusters of 3 or 4 statements or questions that relate to a particular passage of text (from which you must ascertain the answer). SHL tests provide you with a statement that you must then analyse to decide, in light of the passage, whether it is objectively true (based *only* on the passage), objectively false or whether you 'cannot say' either way as the passage has not provided a clear indication. These tests are designed to test your ability to evaluate arguments and statements based on your understanding of a written passage.

Approach

The tests generally require you to *set aside* any external knowledge you may have. This is important to remember! You are thus being tested solely on your ability to interpret text rather than your general knowledge.

I found it useful to begin by slowly and carefully reading the *whole* passage, then tackling each related statement. Whilst answering the first question will therefore take a relatively long time, you should be able to answer the other questions relating to the same passage more quickly. This is because you will know the section of the passage that the statement relates to and will therefore be able to skip sections of the passage that you recognise as being unrelated.

Beware; some passages start with a statement that may indicate the answer is 'true', before later including a statement that determines that the actual answer is in fact 'false' or 'cannot say'. If you simply look at the questions first, then read the passage until you think you have found the answer, you could easily be tricked into making a mistake. Reading the passage slowly and carefully will also ensure you do not overlook double negatives. These can also trip you up or mislead you if you are not really paying attention to each and every word.

Do not fall into the mindset that, because one particular answer has come up a few times in a row, the next answer must surely be something else. For all you know, you got one of the previous answers wrong. Stick with what you think is correct!

Practise

You can sometimes find practice versions of tests on firm websites. Alternatively, you can purchase practice tests from companies that have devised similar tests. Practising can help you to improve your ability to pace yourself, work at speed and familiarise yourself with the format of the tests.

Logical Reasoning Tests

Format

Many City firms use logical reasoning tests produced by SHL as part of their assessment process. Logical reasoning tests typically involve you being presented with a horizontal sequence of 5 images. Each image will be slightly different and the changes in each image give rise to a pattern that allows you to ascertain what the next (i.e. 6th) image in the chain should look like. You will also receive multiple options for what the next image in the sequence could be. Select the one that you believe fits the sequence based on the pattern(s) you have noticed in the original sequence of images that you were presented with.

Approach

Within each image, there will be a number of different elements (typically shapes and/or lines). The key is to first separate (in your mind) each individual element in the first image. One by one, track how each element in turn changes or moves throughout the sequence to ascertain what that element should be in the next (i.e. 6th) image of the sequence.

When you have identified the sequence of changes that occur to the first element (e.g. shape or line) across the images presented to you, look at the potential answers that you are presented with (these are typically in multiple choice form). Which of the possible answers have the element that you have focused upon in the form/position that you would expect based on the pattern(s) you have identified?

There will likely still be multiple options left to choose from, so go back and select another element from the original image, track its movements once again and then check which of the remaining multiple choice options still fit the pattern. Do this until you have only one option remaining. Using a process of elimination can help you to work out which patterns provide a valid explanation for the sequence.

Patterns to look for

The patterns tend to vary and some are more complicated than others (I still come across some that I have no idea how to solve!), but below are some of the patterns you should consider when looking at sequences.

Rotation, position and/or direction

- You may have lines or shapes that rotate or move around the image. Check how often they move/rotate. Are they moving in a particular direction (e.g. clockwise) along a line or around a series of squares? Are their movements triggered by something within the image (perhaps an arrow that changes colour/moves)? Do the movements occur consistently as you progress through the sequence of images (e.g. does every new image have the item in a different position)?

Colour

- You may for instance be presented with some black shapes and some white shapes. Check whether they change colour as you progress through the sequence (e.g. every image or every 2 images).

Number

- You may have elements (for instance shapes or lines) that change in number throughout the sequence. Is there a pattern you can pick up on that dictates when an extra line or shape is added or subtracted (e.g. 1st image: contains 1 circle, 2nd image: contains 2 circles, 3rd image: contains 3 circles)?

Size

- If there are shapes contained within another shape (e.g. a circle containing a smaller triangle and an even smaller square), try to see whether *one* of the shapes from the 1st image reappears in the 2nd image in some form. Does the largest shape in the 1st image (i.e. the circle) become the smallest shape in the 2nd image? Does the shape in the middle of the 1st image (i.e. the triangle) become the largest shape in the 2nd image? If so, such changes may indicate (an element of) the pattern you are looking for.

The pattern may be simpler than you initially suspect. If there are all sorts of shapes and the changes to the shapes across the sequence do not seem to follow any particular pattern, then try looking only at the *colour* or *number* of shapes (or if there is a diagonal line in the middle, then the number of shapes on either side of the line).

Practice

Practising these tests can help you to pick up on the types of patterns that recur more quickly. This is important as the tests are designed to put you under time pressure. Try to get in the habit of quickly zoning out different elements and knowing which patterns to look out for.

Do not panic

The downfall of many candidates undertaking logical reasoning tests is that they panic. When a new set of patterns flashes up on the screen, they may not make any sense for the first few seconds. Keep calm and break down each pattern methodically in order to work towards discovering the answer.

Numerical Reasoning Tests

Format

- Many City firms also use the SHL numerical reasoning tests. These tests tend to present you with tables containing data or graphs, each of which will have a few corresponding questions. Have a calculator, some scrap paper and a pen ready. Most questions will require you to do numerous (but simple) calculations. These tests assess how accurately you read and interpret data, and your *basic* arithmetic capability. Calculations will only usually involve addition, subtraction, multiplication, division and percentages/fractions.

Approach

- Whilst the types of calculations expected of you may be fairly simple, numerical tests tend to put you under extreme time pressure and thus accuracy is key. Your ability to process information quickly and your attention to detail are as (if not more) important than your mathematical ability. For instance, I had not studied Maths for around 7 years when I came across these tests (and am not particularly good with numbers) but still managed to pass many tests, whereas friends of mine doing degrees such as Economics failed a few tests when starting out.

- Tables may contain data relating to various different years, companies, products, sources of income etc. Graphs may contain various different lines or bars that are colour coded to indicate what they are relating to (e.g. different forms of transportation, different products, companies or shares etc.). The axis will also relate to different data (e.g. the year/month, location, value etc. of whatever it is you are being questioned about).

- Start by reading the question *very* carefully and zone out the precise figures from the table/graph that are relevant to the question before making any calculations. This is where scrap paper can come in handy, as you can jot down the relevant information before using your calculator. This can prevent you from accidentally including the wrong information in your calculation.

Situational Judgement Tests

Format

- Situational judgement tests tend to present you with a particular scenario, followed by multiple choice options from which you must choose the option that best correlates with how you would react in the given scenario.

Approach

- When considering your reaction to the scenario, keep in mind the competencies and attitude that the firm testing you is likely to value. If you are applying to a firm in a client-led industry, for a role that involves high expectations and long hours at times, then remember this if questioned on how you would react if you were asked to work late. If you are applying for a role for which accuracy and attention to detail are very important, then bear this in mind if a question is testing whether you would rush through a piece of work if certain circumstances arose.

- However, remember that these tests are designed not to catch you out, but to test your suitability to the firm. If you answer questions honestly and do not proceed through that round of the assessment, then perhaps that firm was not the right firm for you. It may be that your personal qualities and attitude perhaps simply do not fit with the firm's expectations (which in turn could give rise to a miserable working experience).

E-tray / Email Simulation Exercises

Some firms also require candidates to complete an e-tray or email simulation test. These can take many different forms so please bear in mind that this advice is general and you should research into the specific test set by the firm to which you are applying.

Format

- E-tray exercises are typically based within a programme that looks like an email client (such as Outlook), complete with an inbox. Emails typically flow into the inbox over a defined period of time. These emails generally simulate the types of emails you may receive when actually undertaking the role for which you are applying and candidates must respond (accurately) to these emails, usually under time pressure.

- You will probably be provided with ample information from which the answers to the emails can be ascertained. The information in the test I completed was presented in a series of documents contained within folders and sub folders. Some tests are in a multiple-choice format, requiring candidates to choose the answer that is most applicable (and sometimes also the answer that is the least applicable).

- The content of emails could relate to a whole host of tasks. You may be asked about the amount owed by a particular client to date or whom a particular email should be forwarded to. You may have to solve specific problems. You may have to decide how best to delegate a particular task or which emails/issues should be prioritised. You may be required to provide an update on a particular matter. These tests tend to be more specifically designed by/for the firms that set them, so be prepared for anything.

Approach

- Your organisational and time management skills, ability to work under pressure and proficiency using computers are being tested. Employers are also assessing your attention to detail (thus ensure you read and follow any instructions you receive throughout the tests carefully), your ability to interpret ample information in short periods of time, your ability to prioritise and make quick decisions and (depending on the questions) your commercial awareness.

- When completing an E-tray exercise, be sure to keep track of how many emails you have responded to. I forgot to do this once and the test I was doing gave no indication of how many emails I had answered, which meant that I found it difficult to pace myself.

- If you are given reading time, make sure you read all the available documents as you will then know which specific document(s) to reference in order to answer particular questions that are raised. I got bogged down writing notes and only managed to read through around half of the documents provided before emails started flowing in during one test. The test would have been far less stressful if I had taken a different approach.

Converting Internships Into Full-time Jobs

Internships gives firms the opportunity to asses your character and suitability to both the firm and the role in much greater depth. Firms will look at the way you approach work and the quality of work you are able to deliver. Firms will assess how you interact with employees and other interns and how well you are able to work in a team. Firms will look to see which candidates remain enthusiastic and seem genuinely interest in both the firm and the career/work.

We have supplemented the below section with a series of videos relating to converting internships into full-time jobs. These can be found at:

www.CityCareerSeries.com → Internships → Converting Internships

Approaching The Work

- If you cannot do the work to the standard expected by the firm, they will be unlikely to offer you a job. Whilst some pieces of set work will be harder than others, and minor mistakes may be completely fine, general attention to detail should never be overlooked. Proof read your work multiple times (even ask colleagues to have a read if you think this might be appropriate) and make sure there are no spelling, grammatical or formatting errors. These can be easily avoided.

- Check to see whether there are particular fonts, templates or settings in Word or Excel that firms use as part of their 'house style' and where possible, adhere to these. This demonstrates your ability to absorb (and work in a way that aligns with) the ways in which the firm operates, whilst also ensuring the people judging your work will approve of it stylistically. There may also be templates of contracts or spreadsheets that you can edit rather than having to start from scratch. Research and/or ask. You could also see whether the firm has an intranet and/or support departments that can help (e.g. Knowledge Management departments).

- Consider the intended recipient of the work. If it is for a client, then ensure it is short, concise and to the point (unless you are told otherwise) and that the language is not too technical or full of jargon and acronyms. If the work is for a senior employee, perhaps query whether they would like you to reference the work (this means indicating the sources from which you found the information included), whether they have a rough word limit in mind, whether they would like a printed and/or an electronic copy and perhaps even whether they would like single or double sided printing. These are not stupid questions and can help to ensure the work is perceived as favourably as possible.

- Whenever you meet with someone, bring a pad and pen so that you are ready to write down instructions if you are set a new piece of work. Once you have received the instructions, you could summarise them back to your supervisor to check that you have understood them correctly. Ask questions if you are unclear on a particular instruction, but listen carefully. Asking the same question twice will waste your supervisor's time and reflect negatively on you. Try to figure out as much as possible by yourself through researching carefully. You could try to list out questions that arise as you run into difficulties and then ask them all at once when your supervisor has a free moment. Repeatedly interrupting your supervisor every time you have a question could frustrate him or her and disrupt his or her own work.

- Keep a work diary as you go along. You will then be able to reflect back on your previous work if questioned by your supervisor or an interviewer at a later stage. However, do not forget about confidentiality. If you include confidential information in your work diary, then consider refraining from taking it outside the office (during or after your internship). You could alternatively include just enough information to jog your memory about what you were doing, without including confidential client information. When making a job application after completing an internship, never include confidential details of work completed elsewhere. This could call into question your ability to adhere to the required standards of confidentiality.

Group Work & Team Presentations

- Many City careers involve employees having to regularly work in teams. This may be internally within their particular departments; internally within their firm but with a number of different departments that have a role on a different aspect of a deal (for instance the tax or regulatory implications of a transaction); with employees working within a different office within the global network of offices (if the firm is international); and/or with other types of firms. For instance, many transactions involve input from investment banks, law firms, accountancy firms, consultancy firms, regulators and institutional investors and these different industry players must coordinate effectively in order to successfully execute the transaction at hand.

- Internships (and some assessment days) typically include a team-based exercise to test the way in which candidates interact with others on a mutual task. This could involve completing a creative task in a group, for instance building a Lego tower in line with specific instructions. It could involve researching and delivering a group presentation relating to the firm in general or a particular department. This may be structured as a pitch to a fictional client that focuses on the firm's capabilities, its past experience, the challenges it is facing, the locations in which new offices should be opened, or even the way in which it can offer value for money to clients (perhaps addressing fee structures or value-adding services).

- Alternatively, group exercises could involve engaging in fictitious commercial negotiations (sometimes with more than 2 opposing sides) or discussing various investment options as a group before agreeing which one to pursue. These exercises may also be designed to test candidates' commercial awareness and knowledge of the firm.

- Graduate recruiters are very perceptive and are likely to notice if the attitude of one or two candidates adversely impacts upon the team dynamic (even if this dynamic only surfaces when candidates are working together in private). Try to work well with team members. Encourage quieter team members to speak, be receptive of ideas (or constructively contribute to ideas you believe are less strong).

- You could try to link ideas together and draw on others' contributions, arrive at meetings on time and having completed your delegated work and above all, avoid being rude, overbearing or competitive. Candidates who are outwardly competitive are not generally looked upon favourably. Such an attitude can indicate that candidates will negatively impact upon the firm's culture if they were to be offered a job. After all, these exercises are about collaboration, not competition!

- Many presentations are followed by question and answer sessions. If you have worked on a presentation in a team, then make sure you know each other's work and research inside out. You may be allowed to defer an answer to a colleague, but equally you may be expected to answer questions on your colleagues' work. If you are clearly familiar with each other's input then this provides an indication to your assessors that you have worked effectively as a team.

- You may also want to consider supplementing a presentation with a handout. This can enhance your presentation and make your group stand out, whilst also demonstrating creativity, effective teamwork and strong organisation. However, perhaps consider giving out the handout after your speech as it may otherwise distract those in the room from what you have to say.

- Many graduate recruiters claim that there are enough jobs available for a majority of internship candidates if they are all good enough at the work and a strong enough fit for the firm. Acting competitively during group exercises is more likely to lose you an offer than help you to secure one!

Demonstrating Your Motivation

- You are selling yourself during an internship as much as a firm is selling itself to you. Your personality will therefore influence a firm's inclination (or not!) to hire you. They will look for genuine commitment to your chosen career, as they would rather not invest in you, only for you to leave a short way into your career. They will look to see how well you fit in with the firm's culture. Do you get on well with the firm's employees? They will look to see whether you are a hard worker. Have you asked around for work if your supervisor has nothing for you, or have you avoided responsibility or failed to show a genuine interest in the work?

- Your behaviour will influence whether a firm believes you have the ability to complete work in a very demanding, client-led environment and whether you can be trusted to work with high-profile clients and professional services firms that expect only the very best from their advisors and colleagues. Some roles may also require ample confidence and presentation skills. If this is the case, think about whether you are the quiet person in the corner, or the person making an effort to get involved and socialise and how this could in turn reflect on your ability to fulfil the role for which you are applying.

- If you have not received enough work, then request more (you could offer other departments a hand if appropriate). Remember, everything is a learning opportunity, so do not complain if you are set boring or repetitive tasks. You will inevitably receive such tasks at the start of your career if you end up working for the firm in the future. Avoid looking as if you would not be prepared to pitch in and get things done.

Enthusiasm

- Feedback that many rejected candidates receive after an internship is that their enthusiasm for the firm was lacking. It is easy to assume that if you are clever enough to do the work required of you, then surely this should be enough. However, if you do not seem enthusiastic when spending only a few weeks (or months) at the firm, this could give the impression that 6 months or a year down the line, perhaps you will no longer care at all. This could in turn affect the quality of your work, impact negatively upon the teams you work in and adversely affect the culture of the firm. Firms will be less willing to hire someone who may potentially negatively impact the firm's culture. Firms generally perceive their culture as something that keeps employees motivated (and thus from a commercial standpoint, boosts productivity). It's not difficult to smile for a few weeks!

- In addition (although this is merely an opinion and is not necessarily reflective of the way all firms operate), firms may be less willing to make offers if they do not believe candidates will accept. This is partially due to the fact that it will be harder to recruit the required number of people (e.g. schedule the right number of interviews or make the right number of offers) if the firm has no idea how many candidates are likely to accept their offers. A lack of enthusiasm may indicate a candidate will quit after only a short period at the firm, meaning that the money invested in training them throughout an internship and the early stages of their career will be wasted.

- You can demonstrate enthusiasm simply by getting involved in as much as you can. Ask lots of carefully considered questions (to your supervisors, graduate recruitment, people you meet during socials and people that give you presentations). Asking questions can really help to demonstrate your genuine interest in the firm.

- Attend as many social and networking events as possible (although of course do not let this affect the quality of your work if you are facing tight deadlines and avoid drinking too much alcohol!). Attendance at these events can demonstrate your interest in integrating into the firm, getting to know your potential future colleagues (including other interns and existing employees) and contributing to the firm's culture. Repeatedly avoiding such events could indicate that you would perhaps rather be working elsewhere, or that you have little interest in familiarising yourself with the firm's employees or its culture. This in turn may also reflect negatively upon your interest in networking (a skill that is essential to facilitate effective team working, especially when external parties are involved) and your motivation for working at that particular firm.

- However, if there are any cultural circumstances that impinge upon your ability to socialise to the same extent as others (for instance if, during Ramadan, you are due to open the fast at the same time that a social is taking place), then explain the situation to the graduate recruitment team.

Professionalism

- Be open and approachable. Try to meet as many people as you can. This could mean asking to sit in another division for a few hours or simply going for coffees with members of your team.

- Be professional and reliable. It should go without saying, but be punctual (especially following a social event that ended late). Do not be too informal, as this could be mistaken for arrogance. Check what the dress code is before you arrive and remain smart and presentable (even if some of the employees take a more casual approach). This does not necessarily mean you must ignore casual Fridays for instance, but do not show up in shorts and flip-flops simply because you have seen a Partner or Director do so.

- Remember you are making an impression on the entire firm. Treat everyone with courtesy and respect, whether they are your supervisor, the receptionists, the most senior employees at the firm, the secretaries or the cleaners. You are being assessed at all times and you never know who graduate recruitment will approach for an opinion on you throughout/after the internship.

- I have heard stories of interns talking negatively about other interns, not realising that one of the group to which they were speaking happened to be a good friend of that intern from university. Any animosity caused in such a manner can typically be perceived by graduate recruiters, which in my personal experience has not done any favours for those speaking negatively of others. Your fellow interns may well be your future colleagues so treat them well in order to ensure that a positive working relationship ensues in the future.

- I have heard candidates at times talk negatively about other firms to graduate recruitment representatives, presumably intending to demonstrate that the current firm is their preference. This could be a huge mistake. Firstly, bad mouthing other firms could convey a degree of arrogance and suggest that you lack professionalism. Secondly, graduate recruiters tend to move between firms fairly regularly and may well end up at the firm that you were badmouthing before that firm has made their final decision about whether to offer you a job. Two of the graduate recruiters running the final internship that I undertook had worked at other firms at the same time that I had attended open days and internships at those other firms. One had even looked after me on my interview day at a different firm only 5 months earlier!

- Moral of the story? Be careful what you say to your colleagues and to graduate recruiters. Remain professional and do not talk negatively about other people and firms - it does not reflect well on you!

Final / Fast-track Interviews

- Whilst three or four structured reasons for wanting to work at a particular firm may scrape you through an interview to secure an internship, much more may be expected of you in an end-of-internship interview. Having spent a number of weeks immersed in a firm's culture, meeting many employees and engaging in real work, your reasons for wanting to work at the firm will have to be more personal, more substantive and less reliant on graduate recruitment marketing materials.

- Ask yourself whether there was a similar type of personality within the firm. Were there people you particularly enjoyed meeting? Was there a culture that really resonated with you (if so, describe this culture and why it appeals)? Were there pieces of work that you felt were particularly interesting and indicative of the type of work that the firm carries out? Did you attend a presentation on the structure of the training that helped to differentiate the firm from its competitors or suggested that the firm's approach to developing its employees aligns with your preferred means of learning and developing?

- Be ready to discuss the work you have completed in detail and how this work fits in with the wider context of the firm's operations. Prepare some carefully considered questions for your interviewers. These might relate to the firm's culture, its future strategies, the challenges it is facing (or may face in the future), its training or anything else you can think of that demonstrates your genuine interest in working there. If you do ask about the firm's challenges and future strategies however, make sure you have undertaken some related research as you may be asked to express a personal opinion.

- Be prepared to give feedback. What have you enjoyed? What did you not enjoy? How does the firm compare to other firms you have interned at? Has your opinion of the firm changed since your internship commenced? If so, how? What has differed from your expectations and preconceptions?

Succeeding during an internship (Clifford Chance)

What practical steps can interns take to prepare for an internship?

We recommend that you familiarise yourself with the firm before starting an internship. Demonstrating knowledge of the firm's departments, deals, clients, objectives etc. can help to demonstrate that you have a genuine interest in getting to know (and wanting to work for) that firm. Prepare questions for which that you have not been able to find answers elsewhere, as this could be your final chance to ask those questions before potentially having to decide on whether or not to accept a job offer. In particular, if a different firm offers something that you particularly like, your current firm may be flexible enough to offer the same.

What do you assess in particular during vacation schemes and are any of these attributes/capabilities more important than others?

We are assessing you for the qualities we look for in all of our trainees. In particular, we look for candidates that are enthusiastic, willing to learn, bright and *genuinely* motivated by/interested in what we do. These attributes are typically identified in candidates that keep an open mind and try to make the most out of all the opportunities on offer throughout the internship (including their various encounters with our employees).

If you have interned elsewhere (or already have job offers from other firms), make sure you don't let this affect your attitude/willingness to get involved. Doing so could reduce your chances of receiving a job offer from us, which would be a shame – especially if you have decided by the end that we are your first choice!

From a soft skills perspective, we look for effective communication and time-management skills, good attention to detail and an ability to act professionally. This means you should try to communicate clearly, adhere to deadlines, be punctual, triple check any work you submit and dress appropriately. Also, be proactive and use your initiative; asking the right questions (to the right people) and carrying out research to supplement your understanding of particular assignments will reflect positively on you.

Although technical skills are important at this stage to some extent, attitude is by far the best indicator of whether an intern is likely to thrive during our training programme. At the end of the day, if you have successfully progressed through the assessment process, we already know you have the capabilities to succeed; the internship is simply our opportunity to see you in action.

What are the most common mistakes made by, and negative behaviours witnessed from, interns and how can these be avoided?

Recruiters are very good at noticing when candidates have a total lack of enthusiasm and fail to keep an open mind about the opportunities ahead. Try to see the learning opportunity in everything you do, whether this is in the context of learning more about the firm, or learning about a technical area of law or finance. Poor attention to detail also comes up a lot in feedback, so make sure you carefully proofread all the work you submit (and each email you send!).

What attributes/behaviours/capabilities do successful interns tend to exhibit?

The best interns tend to be:

- Highly enthusiastic throughout the *entire* scheme: we can usually detect enthusiasm through an intern's general attitude and friendliness;

- Willing to learn and genuinely interested in the work that the firm carries out: this can be evidenced by the quality of questions they ask and the effort they put in when tackling real work;

- Commercial: a foundational knowledge of the firm's clients and key industries can help to demonstrate this, as can your peripheral understanding of the work you complete during the internship; and (above all!)

- Personable: recruiters are great at noticing how you interact with other interns, the firm's lawyers, support staff etc. We are looking for people that can get on with everyone at the firm - that's what a positive culture is all about.

For more information on Clifford Chance, please visit the below websites or contact the graduate recruitment team at: graduate.recruitment@cliffordchance.com.

www.cliffordchancegraduates.com

Instagram@cliffordchancecareers

Facebook @ Clifford Chance Graduates UK

Twitter @ CCGradsUK

CLIFFORD CHANCE

Careers

Further Reading

Christopher Stoakes is the author that inspired me to set up City Career Series and write this handbook. As a former financial journalist, City lawyer, management consultant and top trainer, he knows the business and financial worlds inside out. His engaging style and ability to explain complex concepts with surprising simplicity meant that his books played a significant role in helping me to prepare for interviews. As such, I strongly recommend that you supplement your study of this handbook by reading some (or all) of the books detailed in this section.

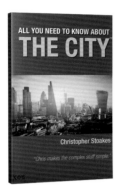

Understand the financial markets

Anyone who works in business these days needs to understand the financial world. All You Need To Know About The City is the best-selling guide that students and young professionals use to get up-to-speed quickly and painlessly. It uses the simple analogy of a market to explain who the participants are (issuers, intermediaries and institutional investors). It looks at what they buy and sell, from shares and bonds to foreign exchange, derivatives and securitisations. It examines the lifecycle of a company and the anatomy of a global bank. It explains why interest rates change and how they drive markets. In short, it enables you to understand the financial markets with no prior knowledge.

Enhance your commercial awareness

If you want a job in the business world you need to be commercially aware. What is it and how do you get it? All You Need To Know About Commercial Awareness tells you. It explains what matters to businesses, how they are funded, the importance of cash flow, the purpose of strategy and the quest for customers. It explains how companies are organised and what they are looking for when you apply for a job. This book contextualises much of the information within this handbook, providing an excellent supplementary read.

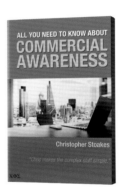

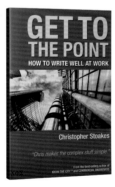

Write well at work

A majority of firms require candidates to submit written assignments as part of the interview and/or internship assessment process. Candidates are expected to write concisely and accurately and frame their words within a clear and coherent structure. However, employers complain that young people can't write. What are they looking for and how can you deliver it? Get To The Point explains how. Writing well in the workplace is critical to your career. Words are still the principal form of communication between people in business. Write well and you will shine. Write badly and you could torpedo your career.

Want to become a lawyer?

Articulating your motivation for wanting to pursue law, both as a degree discipline and as a potential career, is something with which many students tend to struggle. However, firms are increasingly expecting candidates to provide strong, substantial and genuine reasons to support their decision to pursue law. Is Law For You? provides a strong insight into the world of law through explaining both what lawyers do and the many avenues of specialisation they pursue. Whether or not you eventually decide to become a lawyer, law is a critical underpinning to business and thus having a basic grasp of the law will give you an edge regardless.

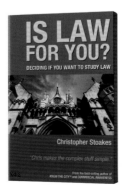

We have produced some additional resources to help you build your commercial awareness. These can be found at:

www.CityCareerSeries.com → Commercial Awareness → Developing Your Commercial Awareness